A HEART FOR AFRICA

A HEART FOR AFRICA

The Story of Jean Nicolson

Missionary in Zimbabwe

Dolina MacCuish

Dolina MacCuish

FREE PRESBYTERIAN PUBLICATIONS

FREE PRESBYTERIAN PUBLICATIONS
133 Woodlands Road
Glasgow G3 6LE
www.fpchurch.org.uk/publications

First published 2008

ISBN 0 902506 63 3

Printed by
Bell and Bain Limited
Glasgow

Foreword

OVER the centuries since the stone was rolled away from the Saviour's grave, women have, in their own sphere, made an inestimable contribution to the propagation of the gospel – the spreading abroad of the fame of Christ as a Redeemer. Even before His glorious resurrection, it is on record that they followed and ministered to Him in life; in death they were last at the cross, last at the sepulchre, and first to return to it as that most auspicious day in this world's history began to dawn. Paul is not forgetful of the women who, in Philippi, laboured with him in the gospel. Priscilla is remembered as having been in Ephesus associated with her husband Aquila in teaching Apollos "the way of God more perfectly". In Joppa we find the industrious Dorcas; while in Cenchrea, Phebe is found labouring as a "servant of the church". These are but a few of the many whose names are in the book of life and whose work and labour of love is not and shall not be forgotten.

We regard Jean Nicolson as worthy of a place in that honourable company. Her lifetime was one of devoted service to the cause of Christ on the Mission of the Free Presbyterian Church of Scotland in Africa. A humble and loving Christian, one would not need to be long in her company to discover that her background and pilgrimage here in time were of no ordinary interest. She doubtless would have shrunk away from the comparison, but those who knew her best might well say that she was of the same disposition as the psalmist: "I will meditate also of all Thy work, and talk of Thy doings." It was assuredly not in any vainglorious manner that she spoke and wrote of the Lord's dealings with her in His holy providence and grace, but it could not be hid that she had a wealth of Christian experience to draw on. And when she was in a reminiscent frame of mind, her ability to command and maintain the attention of her hearers was quite remarkable. She has left a fragrant memory behind her.

Dolina MacCuish's account of Jean's life and labours is written from the viewpoint of one who knew her well and who is familiar with the Mission stations mentioned, having visited Zimbabwe herself on several occasions over the period of time that her sister Ishbel served as a teacher at the John Tallach Secondary School. Her brief biography of Martin Luther's wife entitled, *Luther and His Katie,* and of Augustine entitled, *Augustine, a Mother's Son,* both published by Christian Focus Publications, are already well known and we hope this publication will also prove to be of great interest to all who believe that "the righteous shall be in everlasting remembrance". Of the woman who broke the alabaster box of very precious ointment and poured it upon His head, the Saviour testified that, wherever the gospel would be preached throughout the whole world, her action would be told for a memorial of her. In its own way we hope this book will keep fresh the memory of one who also in the field allotted to her did what she could in the service of the same Master.

JOHN MACLEOD

Contents

er cousin knew by bitter

Acknowledgments

I N writing this short account of Jean Nicolson's life I am indebted both to her relatives and to her "Mission family", as she thought of them, for their interest and encouragement.

Her cousins knew her background as a member of the family and Jean also left notebooks. Many of her Mission friends appear in the text – Catherine, Katie, Ishbel, Marion, William and others and it is to them I am indebted for personal memories of her life on the Mission. They and others – Sheila Macleod, Roddy Campbell, Ella MacRae among them – offered tapes, letters, photographs, magazines. Thanks are due also to Rev John MacLeod who realised that Jean had a story to tell.

My late sister, Flora Chisholm, was the first to offer help, valiantly undertaking to look through magazines and reports, noting relevant information. To my sister, Mary Gillanders and her husband I owe gratitude for their generous hospitality while the book was in preparation. Finally I wish to thank their daughter, Zella, and neighbour, Lynn Singerton, for so willingly giving me the benefit of their expertise with computers.

D O L I N A   M A C C U I S H

● Chapter 1 ●

Norman

JEAN NICOLSON'S life spanned most of the twentieth century. She was born in Tucson, in the American state of Arizona, but her people belonged to the little villages that cling to the jagged coast of Sutherland in the far north-west of Scotland. The blue lochs and heather-clad hills of that rugged landscape formed part of her mental background and as a child she loved to listen to stories about her forebears.

It was in the fishing village of Culkein, ten miles north of Lochinver that her grandparents set up home and in time three children – Norman, born in 1871, Murdo and Sarah – filled the house with laughter and chatter. But sorrow came early to the little family. Both parents died young and the children were taken into the care of their grandmother, Ann Nicolson.

Like many in the Highlands of Scotland towards the end of the nineteenth century, they had the privilege of a Christian upbringing. The Nicolson family belonged to the Free Church and churchgoing was a regular part of life. However busy the week had been – and both men and women worked long hours and hard – when the Sabbath came, there was a stillness and quiet that could be felt. Games and toys were set aside – as were all activities other than works of necessity and mercy – and the family joined the throng of worshippers converging on the church, where the service was conducted in Gaelic, the everyday language of the people.

A recent photograph of the house in Culkein where Norman spent his young days.

In the afternoon the children gathered round while Granny told them stories from the Bible. They perhaps learned a psalm – "I to the hills will lift mine eyes . . ", or "The Lord's my shepherd . . . ". Then Granny would go through the Shorter Catechism with them. She would ask the first question, "What is man's chief end?" The children would recite, "Man's chief end is to glorify God and to enjoy Him for ever." "What rule hath God given whereby we may glorify and enjoy Him?" "The Word of God . . . is the only rule . . . ". and so they gradually came to know question and answer by heart.

Religion was part of everyday life. There was grace before meals, and after. Morning and evening there was family worship when the big Gaelic Bible was taken down from its shelf and it was "eyes shut and hands bonny" as Granny asked a blessing on the Word read. Verses of a psalm were read and sung to one of the old Gaelic tunes – Bangor or Coleshill, perhaps Kilmarnock – all joining in with full-throated vigour. A chapter of the Bible was read, the children perhaps taking turns in reading some of the verses. Finally everyone knelt while Granny led them in prayer.

A HEART FOR AFRICA

When she was no longer fit to cope with three lively youngsters, her son John and his wife Flora took them into their home. Norman's high spirits led him into all sorts of scrapes with the inevitable consequences. After one scolding with accompanying skelp – for nothing much, he told himself – he ran away and got himself a job as a cabin-boy on a small coastal cargo boat. The heady sense of independence soon evaporated. Life on the ocean wave was not, after all, the jolly jaunt he had anticipated – so homeward he trudged to a prodigal's welcome.

Culkein might have been remote from the hub of the nation but there was nothing parochial in the thinking of the crofters and fisherfolk of Assynt. They looked out on an expanse of ocean and knew that in lands beyond the sea their own people had made new homes. From time to time those adventurous ones returned with tales to tell, and when one family had a visit from an uncle or cousin the whole village shared in the rejoicing.

And so it was that Norman enjoyed the wide horizons of those who grow up by the sea. Letters came from Uncle Alastair who had left Culkein as a lad of 14 and was now a sea-captain in San Francisco. One contained the sad news that his wife, who belonged to Stoer, near Lochinver, had died leaving two young children, Ann and Walter.

It is not surprising that the wanderlust early took hold on the youngster. In his late teens he made up his mind to join his uncle in America. First he would have to earn some money, so off he set for Liverpool to join the police force, but he was too young. Time solved that problem and he was eventually accepted.

The young policeman saved every penny and one evening on counting his slowly-mounting fortune, he found that he had all of five pounds! Soon afterwards, as he came in from work, his landlady told him, "I'm taking in another lodger and he's sharing your room." He was disappointed; gone was his precious privacy. As it transpired, it meant also the loss of his precious fare, for one evening he came home to discover that both it and his room-mate had disappeared! There was nothing for it but to write to his uncle. Could he possibly forward his passage-money and he would repay him as soon as he found work? The fare promptly arrived and Norman was on his way to a warm welcome from Uncle Alastair and his new American wife, Frances.

She used to feel sorry for the lonely widower when she saw him walking down to the shops with his two children. Eventually she found herself married to him! They had a baby girl, Grace, who forthwith commandeered the newcomer as her very own slave and shrieked with laughter as he carried her shoulder-high around house and garden.

At that time, about 1890, San Francisco was a small, largely Roman Catholic town which had been settled by the Spaniards in their early trading days. The houses were of wood, ornately built with verandas and balconies in Spanish style, the gardens bright with flamboyant shrubs and flowers.

In no time Norman had found work on a cargo boat. True to form he worked hard and saved hard and his ability was duly noted. When he attained the rank of Second Officer he decided to visit his folk back home. Boy-like, he looked forward to giving them a surprise. Disembarking at the Broomielaw in Glasgow, he took ship for Lochinver and a brisk ten-mile walk took him by late evening to the old familiar door. He knocked. And waited. His uncle appeared. Disguising his voice, Norman said, "I'm looking for a Mr Nicolson. Does he live here by any chance?"

"I'm Mr Nicolson," replied his uncle.

But his grandmother called, "It is Norman! Let him in, let him in!" Norman never forgot that moment. Years later he still spoke of the thrill it gave him that his grandmother had recognised his voice. A round of visits to relatives and friends followed and all too soon it was time to return to the States.

About 1893 he entered the service of the Pacific Coast Steamship Company and was employed on the often-dangerous Alaska run. By early 1900 he had his first command, the *Al-Ki*. The Press reported on his maiden trip: "Captain Nicolson has a host of friends in this city who made him blush like a schoolboy with their congratulations, and the boys gave him an encore when he laid the *Al-Ki* up alongside the dock on a heavy flood-tide without a jar. Capt Nicolson is the youngest skipper under the PCSS Co flag and is one of the most skilful navigators in Alaskan waters." Newspaper photographs of the time show a bright, intelligent face with alert, interested eyes lit by a glint of humour, all suggesting a shrewd judgement and a genial, outgoing personality.

In 1901 he made a further visit to his homeland. He was longing to see his people again and a change of air would do him good, he thought. His grandmother had died but Uncle John and Aunt Flora were still there to welcome him and soon he had settled happily into the routine of the old home. After a few weeks they – or, more probably, his aunt – decided it was time for a little none-too-subtle matchmaking. So his uncle

Captain Norman Nicolson.

announced, "There's a very bonnie girl living near Lochinver. I'll give you a letter to take to her father – and you'll enjoy meeting the family." A twelve-mile hike south along the coast road brought him to the pretty village of Inverkirkaig and the letter was duly delivered. In the kitchen the 21-year-old daughter, Jessie, was busy with household chores when she was called through to meet the visitor from abroad. She came; he saw; he was conquered!

Mission accomplished, Norman returned to America with Jessie's address in his pocket. A regular correspondence ensued, viewed with much unease by Jessie's mother who could not bear the thought of losing her daughter to the States and was not in the least surprised, or pleased, when a diamond engagement ring arrived.

Jessie's father was Alexander Macaskill and her mother Jane Mackenzie. They had five sons – Murdo, Donald, Dan, Bill and George. Murdo, the eldest, would remain in the family home and have seven of a family. Donald was the first to emigrate to Canada, where eventually four of them would make their home. Jessie, born in 1879, was the second of the three daughters. Barbara, the oldest, married and lived in Cape Town and Johan remained in Scotland eventually retiring in Edinburgh.

After working for a short time in a local shop, Jessie was at this time teaching in what was known as a side-school. This was a small school under the charge of a teacher who had no formal teacher-training but was deemed competent by the education authority. Soon after Norman's departure Jessie moved to Edinburgh to be a companion to a Miss Butler, a bishop's daughter who, incidentally, gave her a book, *By the Rivers of Africa,* which was to prove of great interest in the future. She then became governess to the two little daughters of Sir John and Lady Hunter in Bearsden, Glasgow, and so began her connection with St Jude's Free Presbyterian Church in that city.

On his return to the States one newspaper carried the news that Captain Nicolson had returned from a five months' European tour. "He went abroad for the benefit of his health, which he reports is now greatly improved." It went on to describe his impressions of the International Exhibition in Glasgow, in particular his visit to the Art Gallery which he described as "filled with the costliest and rarest works of art . . . from every principal gallery in Europe and America!"

Norman resumed command of the *Al-Ki* and subsequently commanded various ships – the *Cottage City,* the *Oregon* and the *City of Seattle* – all the while gaining valuable experience. Under the headline "Wind Blew Furious Gales", a newspaper reported, "For two days and two nights the wind blew living gales. At times it came with a sweep literally carrying the vessel broadside, temporarily at least rendering it impossible to steer the craft. . . . Coming across Queen Charlotte [Sound], southeast gales which blew with all but hurricane force were encountered all Saturday. . . . Through it all Capt Nicolson displayed splendid seamanship, at no time losing his head. Some of the seamen who have been long on the run say rougher weather was never experienced in these waters."

In 1903 he received a new command. The *Seattle Post-Intelligencer* of 20 May carried the news that Captain Nicolson was to command SS *Spokane,* flagship of the fleet, and commented that

THE SEATTLE POST-INTELLIGENCER. SATURDAY, MAY 23, 1903.

PRESIDENTIAL STEAMER SPOKANE
AND HER CAPTAIN NORMAN NICHOLSON

PHOTO TAKEN IN TAKOU INLET

THE steamer Spokane, which is to convey President Roosevelt about Puget sound, is a modern passenger-carrying vessel. While not as large as some others, she is probably the most comfortable and luxuriously fitted craft running out of this port. She is owned by the Pacific Coast Company, and is operated by the Pacific Coast Steamship Company. The Spokane was especially designed for the Alaska excursion traffic. She is a product of the Union Iron Works of San Francisco. Early last summer she began her excursion runs to Southeastern Alaska. During the season she carried hundreds of excursionists, principally from the East, to and from Alaska. Capt. Norman Nicolson will command the Spokane on her presidential voyage. He was recently assigned to the command of the vessel, having formerly been master of the Alaska steamer City of Seattle. Capt. Nicolson is a young man, though he has long been regarded as one of the safest and most capable navigators on the Pacific coast.

The Rev Neil Cameron – minister at St Jude's Free Presbyterian church, Glasgow, from 1896 until his death in 1932.

though a young man, "he has long been regarded as one of the safest and most capable navigators in the Pacific coast." In the spring of that year he once more visited his native land for several weeks, this time to claim his bride. The wedding was to be conducted by the Rev Neil Cameron, minister of the church in which Jessie worshipped in Glasgow.

Both families belonged to the Free Presbyterian Church of Scotland. This denomination had been formed in 1893, the year after the Free Church General Assembly passed a Declaratory Act which allowed ministers when taking their ordination vows to do so with mental reservations. Rev Donald Macfarlane, minister of the Raasay congregation, tabled a Protest and subsequently with Rev Donald Macdonald of Shieldaig formed the Free Presbyterian Church of Scotland, unreservedly subscribing to the Westminster Confession of Faith. Neil Cameron was one of the divinity students of that time who joined the newly-founded denomination. The Nicolson and Macaskill families were two of the thousands who adhered to it.

On a farewell visit to Inverkirkaig before her wedding, Jessie went to see an old lady known locally as Bantrach Ealasaid (Widow Elizabeth), a fine Christian who lived with her daughter near Lochinver. After tea they went for a walk and as the old lady took Jessie's arm she said, "Well my dear, you are now about to enter on the troubles of life."

"What a strange thing to say to a girl who is about to get married!" protested her daughter.

"Oh, but it's true," she said, "and I want you to learn by heart some words that I hope you will never forget. They are in the seventeenth chapter of the Prophecy of Jeremiah," and she repeated the verses: "Cursed be the man that trusteth in man . . . . For he shall be like the heath in the desert, and shall not see when good cometh . . . . Blessed is the man that trusteth in the Lord, and whose hope the Lord is. For he shall be as a tree planted by the waters, and that spreadeth out her roots by the river, and shall not see when heat cometh, but her leaf shall be green." There and then Jessie memorised the words – and promptly but then forgot all about the incident!

The wedding took place in the Bath Hotel, Glasgow, on Wednesday, 3 June, and soon afterwards the young couple left for America. They settled in Seattle where they bought a small house with four acres of ground. They employed a man to look after the orchard and their Jersey cow while a maid helped Mrs Nicolson with the housework. The little differences from home were intriguing at first and then they were suddenly no longer noticed. A friend showed her around town. "I guess you'll need a spider," she said as they passed a store. "A spider?" queried Mrs Nicolson – but a spider, it seemed, was simply an innocuous frying-pan!

Norman's initial trip on the *Spokane* was a tour of Puget Sound with President Roosevelt on board. The Captain vacated his cabin for the distinguished guest and proudly reported to Jessie that the President

SPOKANE TO SAIL FOR ALASKA

Gets Away Tomorrow on Her First Excursion Trip.

Capt. Nicholson Tells of the Many Pleasant Moments He Spent With President Roosevelt.

The steamer Spokane, Capt. Norman Nicholson, will sail at 9 o'clock tomorrow morning on the first of her series of Alaska excursion tours. On this trip she will visit all of the leading ports of Southeastern Alaska and the various scenic attractions, including the Muir glacier, making the round trip in eleven days.

On this trip, as on each of her five subsequent excursion trips this summer, the Spokane will carry a large number of Eastern and California tourists. Some twenty of these came from San Francisco on the steamer City of Puebla, and others will arrive by train this evening and tomorrow morning. The passenger reservations on the steamer were made at the San Francisco office, so the local agents will not know until tomorrow just how many passengers she will carry. She has first class accommodations for 200 people and will carry no second class passengers, no one way passengers and very little cargo.

Capt. Nicholson enjoys the distinction of having commanded the first merchant vessel from which the flag of the President of the United States was ever floated. He took occasion, while the presidential party was on board his vessel on Saturday to inform himself on this point and can now make the positive claim to that honor.

Capt. Nicholson returns from taking the President and his party around the trip a very warm admirer of Roosevelt. He was very graciously treated by the President and was with him more of the time during the trip than any other man on board.

"President Roosevelt is very well informed on the early history of Puget Sound," said Capt. Nicholson this morning, "and he asked a great many questions regarding the country, the towns we sighted, the channel, the harbors and the navigation of Sound waters. He possesses a fund of general and detailed information which is astonishing to a man meeting him for the first time and his graciousness towards all with whom he came in contact was particularly noticeable. Most of the time he was on the steamer he spent on the bridge or in his own room, meeting or talking with few of the members of the parties on board.

"The President expressed himself very enthusiastically on the subject of the pleasure he derived from the Sound trip, declaring that it was the most enjoyable part of his entire tour. He has been on the ocean several times, having made a number of trips to Europe, and we enjoyed a brief discussion of my own native Scotland, with which country he is quite well acquainted."

had greatly admired a cushion she had crocheted. According to press reports Captain Nicolson returned from the trip "a very warm admirer" of the President, with whom he had enjoyed many interesting conversations.

The *Spokane* was luxuriously fitted out for the Alaska Excursion run. Alaska had been purchased from Russia for four million dollars. It was a rich land and beautiful, the Eldorado of those years, and VIPs and dignitaries from abroad were often offered a visit by the government. Mrs Nicolson accompanied her husband on at least two occasions. On one of these trips a large party of scientists – geologists, botanists, ornithologists – with artists and journalists produced a limited edition of their findings richly illustrated with coloured plates of glaciers, birds, plants and flowers. A copy of each volume was presented to the Captain and these eventually found their way to a grand-daughter of Alastair Nicolson in San Francisco.

Several excursions followed. One passenger describing what was clearly an enthralling voyage wrote, "We were chiefly to be congratulated on our Scotch captain, Norman Nicolson, a superior commander and a delightful host. Next to the command of the ship, his chief concern was the pleasure of the passengers. One evening he invited us to his cabin and, spreading out his charts, explained the great circle and Mercator's sailing. One of the party asked if the compass was ever deflected by iron deposits, and the next day we were sent for to go on the bridge, and there we saw the needle move a degree as we passed an island where there was iron ore." An appreciative testimonial was read to the captain after lunch the day before disembarking; "No intimation had been given, and he was too astounded to respond. Even praise that comes like an avalanche may bewilder a man, but we who sat at his table all the way realised that it was modesty that made him silent and that he was as grateful as though he had made an eloquent reply."

The *Spokane* used to anchor out in the Pacific at some distance from the coast of British Columbia and not far from the island of Metlakatla, where Rev William Duncan looked after his congregation of North American Indians. A Church of England missionary, his mission station had originally been on the mainland but when the gold rush began with its attendant temptations, particularly to strong drink, he transferred his people to Metlakatla. He often came out with some of the Indians on a small fishing boat to meet the *Spokane* and they and Captain Nicolson became firm friends. He told the story of how a converted Indian chief had confessed to him that he had once killed a white man and was greatly burdened by the guilt of this sin. Mr Duncan told him that he must confess his crime to the nearest magistrate who happened to be the commander of a British man-of-war which patrolled the coast. This he duly did. In view of the fact that the crime had been committed in a state of primitive ignorance he was admonished and set free to return to his home in peace.

Perhaps a captain is never completely off duty. One night when Captain Nicolson was sleeping soundly in his cabin he suddenly sat up fully alert. The ship was going through a narrow channel between high cliffs known as The Narrows and he recognised that the ship was in danger. Leaping from his bunk he dashed to the wheel-house and wrenched the wheel from the hands of the quarter-master who yelled, "You'll have us on the rocks!" "We're on the rocks!" was the riposte as the ship was swung clear of the hazard.

With such tales he entertained his wife and, later, his little boy, who was born in December 1904 and named David Mackinlay after a close friend. They attended a Presbyterian church in Seattle and three years passed quickly and happily.

● CHAPTER **2** ●

The Arizona Desert

A s the last member of her family, Jean was anxious that her parents' life should not be forgotten. Her mother must have spoken in detail about her time in America, for when Jean recounted her story it was almost as if she was recalling what she had known at first hand. She was a gifted speaker and could keep her listeners enthralled whether, a few friends around a lunch table or an audience of a hundred.

Her manner of speaking was essentially the same in each setting – matter-of-fact, rather understated, completely absorbed in the telling. Words were crisply enunciated, gestures were few but effective – a turn of the hand, or a sideways glance with raised eyebrow.

What follows is the story of their life in Arizona as told by Jean. It is essentially a spoken account as recorded by one or another of her many friends, and those who knew her will recognise the style. By 1905 her parents were settled in Seattle with little Mackinlay and as Jean put it, "everything was wonderful".

•

One day, my father came home from one of his trips looking very sad, even dejected. One of the young officers had died on the voyage. After telling my mother about it he added, "However, he was a good-living fellow – he didn't smoke and he didn't drink. I think he'll be all right."

"But that's not how you get to heaven," my mother said. She herself at this time was not converted, but she had been well instructed.

"What do you mean?" my father said, surprised.

"It's through faith in Christ that we are saved," she replied.

"Never heard that!" he said. Free Presbyterian!

"Oh but it's true!"

No more was said – but my mother noticed that from that time he began reading his Bible on his own and appeared to be altogether more serious.

Some time later there was a severe storm at sea and my father insisted on being at the wheel for 36 hours. The billows crashed over the deck and it looked as if the ship must go down. However, they did get safely to port. He arrived home with a severe cold in his chest and though he was attending the doctor he didn't seem to be getting any better. So they went to see a specialist. The specialist said, "Young man, you won't live for six months." My mother was shocked beyond words. He had developed tuberculosis, for which at that time there was no cure. "The only thing I can suggest," said the doctor, "is that you go down to the Arizona Desert and live out in the open air

Typical scenery in the Arizona Desert.

and perhaps your health will improve." My mother said afterwards that it was the worst possible thing to do.

However, they packed up and made ready to leave. A caretaker would look after the house for the few months they expected to be away and a neighbour was glad to take the Jersey cow. And off they went by train to Uncle Alastair in San Francisco. Mother at this time was 26 years old. My father was 34 and there was little Mackinlay. They got permission to settle on a ranch in Arizona and set off for Tucson, which was then a small town. They brought with them tents, bedding, crockery, cutlery and a few pieces of furniture. From Tucson they travelled, no doubt by bullock cart, 50 miles into the mountains.

My father secured the services of a Mexican Indian, Juan Tex. He was a great help; soon he had set up the tents. My mother had brought some cretonne and in no time she had the place home-like with cushions and covers and knick-knacks.

But the heat was tremendous – 120°F in the shade. Mother was getting severe headaches; she had very high colour and the heat affected her greatly. It didn't affect my father so much. He used to cheer up my mother up by saying that they would never have seen so much of each other if it were not for his illness. He'd say, "If all's well we'll buy a small place in Scotland and have a horse and cow and chickens just like here."

My mother soon learned to ride the horse and he proved a reliable animal – apart from the time he tossed her into the river! Soon they had a chicken-run. Someone taught her to shoot – it may have been Juan Tex. On two occasions she shot a rattlesnake as it made for the chickens. "I'd never have dared to shoot it," she used to say, "if it hadn't been caught in the netting." A rattlesnake bite was deadly. I still have the rattles from the tails of those snakes. Juan Tex put them into a little glass bottle for her to show to her friends in the future.

Their neighbours on the ranch were Mexican Indians, Roman Catholics. They spoke Spanish. Some, including Juan Tex, spoke a little English. The priest who visited the neighbourhood from time to time turned the people against my parents. For one thing they knew my father had tuberculosis and feared it, and also they knew that they were Protestants. They did everything they could to drive them away. They lamed the horse and beat the cow so that she could not be milked; so my parents had to buy another horse and another cow. But they stuck it out.

Gradually my mother learned to speak a little Spanish and once, when she had gone to the well to fetch water – usually Juan Tex's task – she found two Mexican Indians there. One said to the other, "She is nice-looking!" The other replied, "You should have seen her when she first came here!" Mother was pleased with the compliment and amused – little did they realise that she understood every word!

In the cool of the evening my parents used to sit in the tent door looking across at the mountains in the distance. Aloes, tall and stiff, grew everywhere. They bloomed at various times; some every year, some every ten years, others once in a hundred years. Who was able to check the one hundred years, I don't know – but in the springtime the whole desert was alive with beautiful wild flowers; no grass.

Artists used to come to paint the desert in bloom. They also painted the Mexican Indians in their red blankets and colourful dress. The women made baskets of the finest grasses and decorated them with dyes made from local plants. Some had well-fitting lids. Beads were placed in a little crest on top of the lid and they rattled as the basket was shaken. A large basket, known as an oya, was several feet tall and was used for carrying water. If kept damp it continued to be water-proof. They also made clay pots which allowed the water to seep through. When placed under a bush or hung on a tree, the water in them became very cold.

My father was very lonely and he so enjoyed the company of these artists and the journalists who came to describe the desert, while they enjoyed listening to his tales of the interesting personalities he had met on board ship.

One day Mother was looking across the desert to the horizon when she saw a great big black ball. She said to Juan Tex, "What is that?"

"Oh," he said, "that's a tornado. It'll be here very soon. Go to the nearest Indian house and ask them to let you shelter in one of their huts because everything you have will be blown sky-high; it's coming in this direction."

So Mother asked the woman if we could have shelter in one of her huts and she said, "No!"

And Mother said, "But Juan Tex says that everything we have will be blown away. Would you not give us one of . . . ?"

"No!"

Mother burst into tears. "You'll let my husband in? The children and I will stay outside but you must let my husband in; otherwise he will die."

"All right!" So my mother and Juan Tex began moving the household goods – but Mother said she was finding her teaspoons in the mud for weeks afterwards.

After they had been in Arizona three years, it was obvious that my father was becoming weaker. One evening they were sitting in the tent door, like Abraham and Sarah, looking across the desert. They could hear the mournful whistle of a train in the distance. To my mother all looked desolate on that evening; she felt so far from civilisation.

"You know," she said, "this reminds me of what the good old woman in Lochinver, Bantrach Ealasaid, said to me when I went to say goodbye: 'Blessed is the man whose trust is in the Lord, and whose hope the Lord is. For he shall be as a tree planted by the waters, and that spreadeth out her roots by the river and shall not see when heat cometh but her leaf shall be green: but cursed is the man whose trust is in man for he shall be like the heath in the desert which shall not see when good cometh.' I'm like the heath in the desert; I put my trust in man; I do not put my trust in God."

"Yes, it is indeed a desert," said my father. "There's not even one person who can speak to us about our souls."

One of my uncles came from Canada to visit us, but otherwise we saw no one except the Indians and these visiting journalists and artists.

About this time one of the journalists and his wife came to say goodbye. "We'll see you next year!" they said.

"Oh no," my father replied. "You will never see me again." My mother looked at him in astonishment. "I'll be gone in six months."

"Oh well," said the journalist, "you'll be all right. You've lived a good life; you've been a good example to us all; you didn't smoke and you didn't drink."

My father was very weak but he got up on his elbow and said, "I'll be a sorry spectacle on the Day of Judgement if I die trusting in my own righteousness. I hope to die trusting in the righteousness of Christ." My mother listened in wonder and in grief.

By this time my father was getting weaker and they moved into Tucson where they rented a small apartment. The doctor was in attendance and they had a night nurse to help my mother. My father became unconscious and remained so for two weeks. My mother was sitting beside him when he recovered consciousness.

"Where are we?" he asked.

"We're in Arizona," my mother replied.

"What are we doing here?"

"You've been ill."

"How long have I been ill?"

"Four years," she said.

"Four years! Well, it's time I prepared to meet the Lord. Read the fourteenth chapter of John!"

She read; "Let not you heart be troubled: ye believe in God, believe also in me. In my Father's house are many mansions: if it were not so I would have told you. I go to prepare a place for you. . . ." And, as she read he passed away.

"Oh," my mother said long afterwards, "I prayed that I would die too. I'd looked after your father all these years. I didn't want to live any longer. But what a mercy the Lord didn't answer that prayer – I was not prepared to die. It wasn't a proper prayer anyway!"

•

Captain Norman Nicolson died at 12.30 pm on Friday, 22nd January, 1909 and was buried in Tucson, in the wide, palm-fringed City Cemetery with the grey-blue hills beyond. Rev Mr Breckenridge conducted the funeral service.

Tributes in the American press spoke of his Christian faith, of his "numerous loveable traits" and of his skill as a mariner. "His record shows him to have been a man of exceptional courage and foresight, and during his 15 years of service as voyager, he never encountered a disaster of any kind through his vessels. He is described as a man of superior knowledge of the Pacific coast and of her steamships. Being of a very genial disposition, he quickly made and retained friends."

Tucson City Cemetery, where Norman Nicolson is buried.

With four-year-old Mackinlay and baby Jean, just past her first birthday on 8th January, Mrs Nicolson set off for San Francisco where Uncle Alastair, hospitable as ever, offered her his home for as long as she wished to stay.

● CHAPTER 3 ●

To Scotland

IN San Francisco letters from Mrs Nicolson's mother kept arriving, all urging: "Come home to Scotland!" So a rather forlorn trio set off on the long journey to Inverkirkaig in south-west Sutherland, where they were to make their home for the next five years.

Inverkirkaig is a little seaside village three miles south of Lochinver in the parish of Assynt, a singularly beautiful land of tumbling streams and waterfalls, busy little harbours and spectacular

The MacAskill family home at Inverkirkaig in 2008.

sunsets. Wild flowers carpeted the moorland and nestled in crannies on the lower slopes of the towering crags beside deep lochs. It was a safe and happy environment in which to bring up children. With a granny and uncles and aunts and cousins – Uncle Murdo with his family lived nearby – and neighbours to take a warm and practical interest in them, the fatherless children felt secure and cherished. Not that they were allowed to forget their father; their mother kept his memory fresh in their minds.

Mackinlay was soon enrolled in the local school and when Jean was five she and her friend next door were admitted to the infant class. Every morning the two little girls set off hand-in-hand on the three-mile walk to school in Lochinver. There Jean made a discovery. Everybody had a middle name – or even two – everybody except her, and she felt deprived. So she decided to confer one on herself and after due consideration wrote, in her best writing, "Jean Arizona Nicolson". Some time later her granny picked up a book with the inscription, "This book belongs to Jean A Nicolson", and Jean heard her call to her mother, "I didn't know Jean was called Ann – after Norman's grandmother?"

Schooldays were as happy and carefree as they should be. And out-of-school days were long and full – chasing, climbing, exploring, guddling in rock-pools or simply standing, hands behind back, watching men at work. There was always something doing; a neighbour was repairing the thatch on his barn; another was building a dry-stone dyke; there was the seasonal ritual of clipping and dipping of sheep. In spring the "big boys" would have a fortnight or so off school to help with the potato-planting and again in October they would be similarly privileged, this time to help with harvest. Haystacks were great fun – for the children! In spring peat was cut, laid out to dry, and in summer it was carted home and neatly stacked at the house-end. Life was full of surprises – a hen clucked importantly as she led her little yellow brood from their hiding-place in the bracken; a black-nosed lamb had lost its mother and had to be hand-fed. All this and "the fishing" too!

The women's work was truly never done. Baking scones on the griddle, making butter and crowdie, and fetching water were daily tasks. Washing clothes was almost a day's work. When the clothesline was full, sheets and towels were spread out on bushes. They were taken in wind-dry and blossom-fresh and the ironing began. There was the flat-iron that Granny propped up in front of the grate till it was just the right heat, and there was the box iron; it had a little door at the back. Granny took out the special stone that was inside the iron and put it into the fire. A little later, with the shining brass tongs she lifted it out and slipped it back, glowing hot, into the iron and shut the door. There was a goffering-iron too, for crisping up the frills on the mutches that the older women wore. All that and helping on the croft!

The Sabbath day was different, a therapeutic calm and rest from the busy-ness of the week. A hush was over the land, broken only by the sounds of psalm-singing, the bleating of sheep, the call of a gull, the voice of the wind. . . . Morning and evening, children and parents, "drest in best", walked sedately to church in Lochinver. Sometimes Jean and Mackinlay had the joy of riding in Uncle Murdo's gig pulled by two horses.

When Jean was almost six years old, Mrs Nicolson decided to find work in the south and the family, including Granny, moved to Glasgow. There Mrs Nicolson enrolled in the College of Domestic Science, gaining a First Class Diploma and a teaching qualification. On graduating she took up a post in Johnstone near Glasgow, running a canteen for the firm of John Laing. His son was about to be married and Mrs Nicolson was delighted to meet his fiancée – none other than a daughter of Sir John and Lady Hunter, one of the little girls she had taught years before in Bearsden. She was later employed as a demonstrator with Glasgow Corporation Electricity Showrooms and wrote *Mrs Nicolson's Electric Cookery Book,* which went into three editions.

At first they stayed in what Jean later described as "a modest flat in Partick – two rooms and a kitchen", but in Johnstone a bungalow with a garden was provided at a low rent. She remembered her mother as being always busy. "I hardly saw my mother when I was young except on Sabbaths, and I thought that everyone's mother was tired – my mother was tired all the time. When she was at College she would be up till two in the morning studying science, the subject she found most difficult. Then when we were in Johnstone, after a

Mrs NICOLSON'S
Electric Cookery BOOK

CONTAINING OVER 200 RECIPES
TEMPERATURES & OTHER VALUABLE
INFORMATION SUITABLE FOR ANY
ELECTRIC COOKER

2'6

The front cover of Jessie Nicolson's cookery book, third edition.

day's work she would travel to Glasgow to teach evening classes, coming home at half-past ten at night. We were in Johnstone for five years and then moved to Glasgow."

Mrs Nicolson was once more attending St Jude's Free Presbyterian Church in Blythswood Square, Glasgow, where Rev Neil Cameron was minister. One day, as he preached from the words, "Thou art not far from the kingdom of God", she realised suddenly that she was not in the kingdom and that this became a prime concern with her. It was at this time that Psalm 23, "the shepherd Psalm", became of special significance to her. She became a member of the church in 1931.

The large congregation was mostly working-class and mainly people from the Highlands – young men who had come to find work in the shipyards of the Clyde, on the railway, in factories and offices and who had married and settled in the city, and young women working as housemaids and cooks in what they termed the "big houses". Many of them were highly intelligent and trustworthy so that they were generally much appreciated by their employers. Mr Cameron used to say that it was the pennies these girls put in the collection plate that kept the Church going in the early days when it was very poor and struggling.

St Jude's was an imposing edifice with a

St. Jude's Free Presbyterian church, West George Street, Glasgow – photograph taken in 1974. The congregation moved to Woodlands Road in 1975.

congregation of over a thousand. At the morning and evening services on the Lord's Day the church was packed. Sometimes there was an afternoon service and there was a midweek prayer meeting. The minister, an earnest and thoughtful preacher, made a deep impression on his hearers and won the respect of a wider Christian community. The services were usually conducted in Gaelic and would last at least one-and-a-half hours. Prayers were extempore. The singing, unaccompanied and led by a precentor, was memorable – a slow-swelling cadence as several hundred voices rose and fell, enriched with grace-notes and part-singing. Often the precentor would "put out the line" when the singing was in Gaelic; this custom dated from a time before universal education, when many could not read. The precentor would sing the psalm line by line with the congregation repeating, the whole blending together in a unified chorale.

Jean was more than a little in awe of her minister. Dignified and grave though he was, he knew how to capture a little girl's heart. The offer of a pan drop did the trick. From that moment he was her hero, and her regard for him grew with the passing years.

One day, as Jean and her mother were shopping in Glasgow, a lady in the picturesque uniform of the Salvation Army asked them for directions. Mrs Nicolson gave her the information she required.

"Thank you." Then the lady smiled at Jean: "And do you, my dear, know the way to heaven?" The exchange made an impression on the wee girl and she kept thinking about it.

In Glasgow Mackinlay attended Allan Glen's School while Jean went to Hutchesons' Grammar School for Girls where her special friend was Mary Gatherar; their friendship lasted into adulthood. Jean was already showing her talent for making friends. In sending her children to fee-paying schools and ensuring that Jean had piano lessons, Mrs Nicolson was at that time unusual in her circle.

There was an English-speaking Free Presbyterian congregation in Carlton Place, Glasgow, under Rev James Sinclair, who had a large and lively family of six daughters and three sons. Jean was particularly friendly with Rachel. Between the two congregations there was much scope for making friends. The men had a debating society and there were picnics and general socialising.

A HEART FOR AFRICA

On leaving school Mackinlay decided to be a sailor like his father and joined the merchant navy. While an apprentice on the steamer *Cabotia*, he was awarded a gold medal by the US Government for his part in rescuing the crew from a stricken American ship. A photograph alongside a newspaper account of the presentation ceremony shows a well-built, strapping young man.

Jean's choice was to go, with her friend Mary, to Glasgow University, where she took an Arts course, specialising in English and Celtic. She began a diary on 6th October 1928, at the beginning of her second year at University. The entries would appear to be either summaries of the sermons she heard or the parts that were the most meaningful to her.

Interestingly, the first entry refers to the visit in 1921 of Rev Neil Cameron and Mr Angus Fraser to the Southern Rhodesia Mission of the Church, which Mr Cameron pronounced "really the most enjoyable experience we ever have had; for it gave us the clearest possible proof of the wonderful effects of the gospel among this people." He described how in the cool of the evening they had

A view of Glasgow University, where Jean Nicolson graduated MA in 1931.

listened to the pleasant sound of psalm-singing from the African huts. Jean comments, "Mr Cameron has a warm affection for the Africans since he became acquainted with Rev J B Radasi and since he visited our Mission."

Rev N Cameron preached in Gaelic and English to his own congregation and Jean understood and wrote Gaelic. In her diary there is the occasional quote in Gaelic but even when recording a Gaelic sermon she usually does so in English. Though she makes few personal comments about herself, excerpts from her diary give an indication of the tenor of her thoughts at this time.

•

Oct 8th '28: "So walk ye in Him." To walk in Christ is . . . not to find oneself becoming better and better, day by day, but to find one's need of Christ more and more daily."

Gaelic Prayer Meeting: "It is my opinion," said Mr Cameron, "that men do not pray sufficiently to the Holy Spirit, for He is God, equal in power and glory with the Father and the Son, and to Him is given the work of applying the redemption purchased by Christ to the heart of the sinner. Pray earnestly and continually. Should you find your heart full of all manner of folly and vanity and your thoughts in the end of the earth, persevere in prayer. Although you should find little to say, tell Him of your helplessness. Though your heart should be hard and unrepentant, if you are conscious of it the Lord will hear your prayer and will answer it in His own time."

Dec 5th '28: The natural heart of man supposes God to be an austere being, reaping where He has not sown, gathering where He has not strewn, but that is a carnal thought. God is full of mercy, and pity and love towards poor sinners as we see in the text: "God so loved the world, that He gave His only-begotten Son, that whosoever believeth in Him should not perish, but have everlasting life." You cannot be too great a sinner to come to Christ.

Jan '29: What is God's mercy? It is a deliverance and a complete salvation through Jesus Christ, that we may rejoice and be glad all our days.

Jan 8th midnight '29: My Birthday. Mr Cameron told the story of a godly woman in Strathdearn. A man stood outside her door and heard her give fervent thanks to God for all His goodness in providing for her daily needs. The man entered the house and found her with a cake of Indian meal and a cup of cold water. "Surely you are very thankful," he said, "and you have not very much." "Oh you do not know what I have," said the old woman. "I have Christ with this." So will Christ make sweeter than honey ordinary bread to the true Christian. All things in Providence will have a new aspect.

Feb 29th: Mr Sinclair spoke at night on "The hope of the hypocrite shall perish." I never heard Mr Sinclair preach better and he gave detailed directions on how to detect hypocrisy in one's own breast.

Wednesday: Granny ill.

The Rev James S Sinclair, minister of John Knox's congregation, Carlton Place, Glasgow. He was also editor of the Free Presbyterian Magazine from May 1896 until his death in 1921.

March 18th: No mere man poured out his heart as David did at the end of the 72nd Psalm, when he desired that the glory of Christ should fill the whole earth, as it will do some day. You will notice that it is addressed to the people, "Ye people"; that is, everyone of us individually. It is our duty to do it and not to despair, for He is a God that delighteth in mercy. Lord, give me grace to plead for mercy, only for Christ's sake, believing that Thou art the rewarder of them that diligently seek Thee. I remember Mr MacIntyre saying that grace was as free as the streams that run down the hills in the Highlands, and yet we take the fresh water freely without a thought, but we refuse grace and Christ.

March 30th: Mr Cameron told a story of a minister's experience that he had read somewhere. Every Sabbath morning this minister saw a little ragged boy standing in the passage listening attentively to the sermon, but as soon as the service was over the little boy ran away and the minister could never find out who he was. One day, a man as ragged as the boy called at the manse and asked to see the minister. He told him that he had a little boy who was very ill and earnestly desired to see the minister. "He is a very strange boy," said the man, "and I cannot understand very often what he is saying. I offered to get any other body nearer us but he would have none but you, although we are six miles from here. Will you come and see him?"

The minister went and entered a hovel as poor as their clothing. Inside, on some straw, lay the little ragged boy, and when he saw the minister he lifted up his arms and said, "His right hand and his holy arm hath gotten Him the victory," and he immediately passed away.

"Probably," Mr Cameron said, "that would comfort the minister's heart if he felt his ministry was blessed to the boy and was bringing forth some fruit. The story is to be remembered by little children, for it shows that Christ is ready to save them as well as grown-ups. May our children be led by the Holy Spirit to give their hearts to Christ."

[A plaintive entry]: I wish I was at the prayer-meeting tonight.

April 29th: Mr Cameron: An African, a converted man and suffering under a temptation, prayed, "Lord, take care of Thine own property." He had given himself entirely to Christ.

April 18th: Now to take another plan since thine own has failed and, instead of troubling thyself about evidences, look to Christ! Keep thine eye fixed on Him; meditate on the divinity of His person, the sufficiency of His atonement, the perfection of His righteousness, the riches of His grace, the universality of His invitations. Look at the object of faith, the grounds of faith, the warrant of faith; the more thou dost this, the stronger thy faith will become and the stronger thy faith is, the greater thy peace will be. Instead of labouring to love Christ and becoming dejected that thou dost not love Him more, take another course and dwell upon the love of Christ to thee. It is a great principle which I am anxious to impart upon you: that subjective religion or, in other words, religion in us, is produced and sustained by fixing the mind on objective religion, or the facts and doctrines of the Word of God.

Sept. 11th '29, [one of the last entries surviving]: Isaiah 35: Strengthen ye the weak hands that cannot lay hold on Christ, the weak knees that cannot walk although Christ is saying, "Whosoever cometh unto Me I will in no wise cast out." They cannot come to Him of themselves. Often God's true people are faint of heart and afraid that they never had grace; the world never has these fears.

[There are quotations from Guthrie's *The Christian's Great Interest,* and this from one of the Bonars]; "If any of you ask, 'What is great faith?' the reply is, 'Having a great opinion of Christ. . . . .' Learn to read your title to the family of God by what God has said, not by a special message to yourself."

•

Above: Rev Malcolm Gillies, for 20 years pastor of Stornoway F P congregation. A warm-hearted, humble Christian and an able and edifying Gospel preacher.

Below: Rev Donald Beaton, Oban. Mr Beaton became author of the Free Presbyterian Magazine and the Young People's Magazine and was the author of several books.

Such were Jean's concerns during her early twenties. Rev Malcolm Gillies, Free Presbyterian minister in Stornoway, had a great influence on her, as had Rev Donald Beaton, Oban. She once said, "Mr Cameron preached a lot about faith. Mr Beaton came and he preached Christ." She found that helpful.

She made a profession of faith in Christ in Glasgow about that time, and when she sat at the Lord's Table for the first time, she felt rather downcast. After the service, a lady approached her and said that this was a not unusual experience. Before going to bed that night she read Isaiah, chapter 56. Verse 3 impressed her: "Neither let the son of the

stranger, that hath joined himself to the Lord, speak, saying, The Lord hath utterly separated me from His people: neither let the eunuch say, Behold, I am a dry tree." The following Wednesday evening she heard Rev M Gillies preach in Clydebank on that very text and she was encouraged.

Though Jean had a wide and informed interest in Christian matters she did not speak much about her own experiences; like many of her generation, she was reticent, concerned rather to do what was right in all areas of her life. This integrity became perhaps a defining characteristic.

On 6 June 1931 she graduated MA, and the following year she attended Jordanhill College of Education where she gained a teaching certificate with an endorsement in domestic science. These were the years of the Depression, which threw thousands out of work, and the teaching profession was affected no less than others. Graduates were glad to find work of any kind. Jean obtained various temporary posts and spent two months in Bunavoneader, a village four miles from Tarbert on the island of Harris in the Hebrides assisting the local

Jordanhill College of Education – now part of the University of Strathclyde.

A HEART FOR AFRICA

Glasgow Provincial Committee for the Training of Teachers.

CLASSES FOR THE FURTHER TRAINING OF TEACHERS.

SESSION 1932-33

COURSE No. 1064 G. IN **NEEDLEWORK** (....Second........COURSE)

HELD AT GLASGOW TRAINING CENTRE

It is hereby certified that

JEAN NICOLSON

a Certificated Teacher in - - - - - - - - - -

School, attended the above-named Course, that she

received........60..........hours of instruction out of a possible

........60........ in accordance with the Syllabus on the back

of this Certificate, that....she.....satisfactorily performed

the work of the Course, and obtained the final mark

FAIR PLUS

Teacher of Subject.

George A. Burnett

Director of Studies.

teacher, Mrs Macdonald, a widow from Tomatin near Inverness. She maintained a life-long friendship with the Cameron-Mackintosh family, of which Mrs Macdonald was a member.

By the end of her spell there her thoughts were turning to Africa. She was an avid reader, and quiet Sabbath afternoons gave an opportunity to read a wide range of religious books. Many Highland homes were well stocked with books – by the Erskines, Thomas Boston and Robert Murray M'Cheyne, to name a few. Missionary biography was her favoured reading and she especially enjoyed Robert Moffat, David Brainerd and Henry Martyn. Throughout her life Jean read and re-read such books.

> **Jewish and Foreign Mission Committee Appeal for a Female Teacher for South Africa.**—The Jewish and Foreign Mission Committee had reluctantly to give up the idea of sending a Male Teacher to take charge of their schools in South Africa. This decision had to be taken on account of financial conditions laid down in the Native Development Act passed by the Rhodesian Government. These conditions were unknown to the Committee until the Rev. John Tallach arrived in this country. The Committee would now appeal for a Free Presbyterian Female Teacher who has her certificates in ordinary teaching and Domestic Science. This is a great opportunity for one who has a mind to help in advancing the kingdom of Christ among the native people of Africa. As this matter is pressing, application should be sent in as soon as possible to the Convener, Rev. Neil Macintyre, 4 Warrender Park Crescent, Edinburgh.—Neil Macintyre, *Convener.*

The monthly *Free Presbyterian Magazine* carried interesting letters and reports by the Rev J B Radasi, Rev John Tallach and Rev Dr Roderick Macdonald of the Church's Mission in Southern Rhodesia. Each in his own way had the gift of combining the larger picture with telling detail. The annual reports were positive; the difficulties they encountered did feature but were not dwelt on. It was a young church with a young mission and there was a general enthusiasm and sense of involvement. Church and Mission were struggling to establish themselves. Following their Protest in 1893, Revs D

Macfarlane and D Macdonald had been compelled to leave both church and manse. Consequently many congregations had for a time worshipped in the open air. Churches and manses had to be built both at home and on the mission field with scarce resources; so there was much sacrificial giving of money and energy.

The *Free Presbyterian Magazine* of December 1932 carried an appeal for a teacher with a domestic science qualification to serve in Southern Rhodesia. The term of service would initially be five years followed by one year's paid leave, and an annual salary of £200.

Jean offered her services.

CHAPTER 4

Mission Beginnings

JEAN was, of course, familiar with the history of the Free Presbyterian Mission in Africa.

From its inception the Free Presbyterian Church had been mission-minded; a Foreign Mission Fund was set up in November 1898 and seven years later a Foreign Mission Committee was formed. In 1904 the first missionary had been ordained and was soon to be evangelising among the Matabele in what was then known as Southern Rhodesia. Rhodesia was named in honour of Cecil Rhodes who played a leading part in its establishment as a British colony.

Mzilikazi was the founder of the Matabele who, like the related Zulu and Xhosa, had their origin among the Bantu of the Congo. Over the centuries they had migrated southward and by the early nineteenth century the Nguni Bantu were in the Natal province of Southern Africa. There was much inter-tribal warfare. Chaka, the mighty Zulu warrior was sweeping all before him, earning the accolade "the African Napoleon". As he pressed relentlessly onward Mzilikazi, who had already defied him, deemed it prudent to get out of his way and in 1820 led his followers westwards over the forbidding Drakensberg Mountains into the Transvaal, where they soon subdued the resident Sotho tribes. Fighting was their life, and Mzilikazi organised them into what became, in effect, a formidable fighting machine. He owed much of his success to the fact that he copied Chaka in his use of the assegai, a short spear, and of the circling pincer-movement known as "the horns of the bull" but, unlike Chaka's, his warriors carried distinctive long cowhide shields.

The Matabele were a fierce and energetic race, glorying in their might, raiding and generally harrying their neighbours. Eventually they settled in Northern Transvaal.

European powers were competing for land and influence; hunters, colonists, slave-traders, explorers and prospectors jostled one another. For 20 years Britain and Holland had been engaged in a tug-of-war over Cape Colony and in 1814 the Dutch surrendered their claim on receipt of six million pounds sterling. In 1835 began the Great Trek which saw 14,000 Voortrekker Boers make their way northwards from the Cape across the Orange River and on to the Transvaal. Thus they came into conflict with Mzilikazi and his Matabele followers who were no match for the white man and promptly moved north to the wide plains across the "great, grey-green, greasy Limpopo River" where they subdued and absorbed the peaceful Makaranga. Mzilikazi eventually made his capital at Nyathi, near Bulawayo, which at that time was little more than a huddle of huts.

It was in 1829 that this fierce despot first met the Scottish missionary, Robert Moffat. For almost 30 years he had been in Africa under the auspices of the London Missionary Society and had established a mission station at Kuruman in South Africa. Mzilikazi had heard of the wonderful fields of corn, the orchards, the vegetable plots – an oasis of order, peace and plenty – and sent a delegation to see if all he had heard was true. It was and more! The messengers then persuaded Moffat to go with them to the king's village. The friendship which developed between the lauded "eater of nations, consumer of men" and the mild-mannered preacher whom Mzilikazi called Baba – Father – is one of the most intriguing in missionary history. On a subsequent visit in 1840 Moffat treated the warrior's dropsy – good reason for him to value his friend though he would have none of the missionary's Christianity, even forbidding his people to become Christians on pain of death.

Moffat paid further visits in 1857 and 1859, when his son, John, accompanied him. They requested permission to start a mission in

Matabeleland. After a trial of patience this was finally granted and a station was opened in a valley near Nyathi, where John Moffat settled. Another station was established at Hope Fountain. Even after 20 years there were no converts, but the missionaries, undaunted, laboured on. In September 1868 Mzilikazi died, still a heathen. "The mountain has fallen!" they said. He was succeeded in 1870 by his son Lobengula, who made Bulawayo his capital.

Robert Moffat's daughter, Mary, married the missionary doctor David Livingstone from Blantyre, a village in the south of Scotland. He waged a determined crusade against the Arab

The statue of David Livingstone at Victoria Falls.

slave trade, "that open sore of the world". In his journeys of exploration, with the aim of opening up the continent to trade and missionary endeavour, he came upon the awe-inspiring Mosi oa tunya, – the thundering smoke. This was in November 1855; he called the falls after his queen, Victoria.

As the British continued to expand northwards, the Anglo-Zulu Conflict came to a head in 1879. At Isandlwana on 22nd January a confident British Army – confident because of their superior weaponry – faced 20,000 Zulu warriors and suffered a shattering and humiliating defeat trapped by the "horns of the bull". That same day at Rorke's Drift the situation was reversed when a small British contingent saw off an overwhelming Zulu force. The British stepped up the campaign and six months later were in control of southern Africa.

While David Livingstone laid the foundations on which future mission work would build, Cecil Rhodes made every endeavour to extend British influence in Africa. He had come to the continent in 1870 for the sake of his health and amassed a fortune from gold and diamonds at Kimberley in South Africa. He became increasingly involved in politics, eventually becoming Prime Minister of Cape

"Mosi oa tunya" – the thundering smoke – Victoria Falls.

Colony in 1890. The scramble for Africa had begun. In 1888 Lobengula agreed to the Rudd Concession, which granted Rhodes, acting on behalf of the British Government, sole right to prospect for minerals. In order to exploit the possibilities thus gained and to expand British rule ever northward, he encouraged white people to settle in the country. In 1890 the Pioneer Column of prospective settlers with Selous, the renowned English hunter as guide, hacked its way 400 miles through near-impenetrable jungle and across the open grassy plateau beyond to the territory north of Matabeleland. He planted the Union Jack in Salisbury, which became the capital of the new British colony of Mashonaland. Mines were opened and farms were developed.

Inevitably war broke out between these European settlers in Mashonaland and the neighbouring Matabele. After fierce fighting the Matabele were defeated in 1893 at Gadade near the Ingwenya River – about 30 miles north-east of Bulawayo, and close to where Jean Nicolson was to spend much of her life. Lobengula fled and died a few months later, the last king of the Matabele. Sir Ralph Williams, acknowledging his considerable abilities, wrote that "he always protected the whites". Wisdom dictated that he keep good relations with them. Shrewd and more moderate than Mzilikazi, he knew that with well-armed troops they could in the long run impose their will. Like his father he trusted Moffat and the missionaries, ordering, "Don't let these vessels be broken!" Among those wounded in the fighting was one of Lobengula's bodyguards who came to be known as Isaiah Nyathi.

White settlers now moved into Matabeleland, and Southern Rhodesia was born, comprising the territories of Mashonaland and Matabeleland. In both areas, however, continuing unrest led to an uprising against the white rulers. Rhodes and the Matabele met in the Matopo Hills, near Bulawayo in 1896 to thrash things out. A peaceful settlement was negotiated. It is interesting that the last surviving wife of Mzilikazi acted most effectively as go-between. And among the combatants in that last rebellion was a young Matabele, Ndiyamabombo, also known as John Mpofu. Like Isaiah Nyathi's, his life was to take a turn he could never have imagined.

As a counter to the warlike Matabele, Rhodes invited Fingos from Cape Colony to Matabeleland. A more civilised and peaceful people than the Matabele, they would be a moderating influence on them, he hoped, and might act as a buffer between them and the Europeans. It was a forlorn hope; the two groups had different customs as well as different languages and did not really interact. Many of the Fingos spoke a little English and were friendly to Britain. They too had fled south before Chaka and, about 1824, had settled on the east of the Cape, where they acquired the reputation of being an intelligent, hardworking people, skilled in agriculture and with a thirst for education. By 1880 half of them were reckoned to be Christians.

Rhodes died in 1902. It was to this land that the Free Presbyterian Church was to send its first foreign missionary. John Boyana Radasi, a Fingo, was born about 1876 in Seymour, a small town in Transkei, Cape Colony, and grew up in a Christian home. His father had become a Christian through the influence of the early missionaries and was himself a preacher. He worked for the Government as a court interpreter and was also responsible for mail deliveries between Seymour and Readsdale. He owned 40 acres of land and, as an educated and literate man, he was able and glad to give his son a good education. John spoke fluent English and in his late teens he went to America as a member of a choir in connection with Queen Victoria's Diamond Jubilee due to be celebrated in 1897. There he was converted and made friends with James Saki, also from South Africa and a Christian. The two decided to go to Scotland – a land where, they had heard, the gospel was preached. In the time-honoured way of cash-strapped youth they worked their passage and, landing at Leith, they arrived eventually in Edinburgh in 1896.

The Rev J B Radasi – the first Free Presbyterian missionary in Africa.

One day, as they stood rather uncertainly in the city's Lothian Road, they found themselves being addressed by a complete stranger who explained that he had spent some time in Africa. While visiting his mother, who lived "just across the street there", he had been idly looking out of the window and had spotted the strangers. Would they care to share a meal with him? And that was how the Church acquired its first missionary!

When it transpired that they were two godly young men, Mrs Sinclair contacted Rev Neil Cameron as she knew the Church was interested in starting mission work. This was a mere three years after the Church's beginning. With limited resources, churches and manses required to be built and ministers trained, yet this responsibility was gladly undertaken.

James Saki joined another denomination in 1900, but John Radasi remained with the Free Presbyterian Church and trained as a teacher and a minister. On 16th November 1904 he was ordained to the ministry and subsequently sailed for Africa.

After a short stay with his married sister in Capetown he made for Bulawayo, for it was his ambition to preach the gospel where it had never been heard; also, since the Fingos and Matabele were both branches of the Zulu race, there was a similarity between their languages. When he alighted at Bulawayo, a boom frontier town which had sprung up around the ruins of Lobengula's kraal, he was befriended by a fellow-African, a Wesleyan minister, who approached the stranger and in course of conversation offered him the hospitality of his home till he should be settled. A young Fingo porter, Stephen Hlazo, overheard the conversation and, when he went home at the weekend to Bembesi, 30 miles north-east of Bulawayo, he reported the incident to his father. John Hlazo was an educated man and a Christian, who had at one time been a driver on a mail van and had known Cecil Rhodes personally. He was immediately interested. The upshot was that he and some friends went in search of Mr Radasi and invited him to settle among them, subject to Chief Ngege's approval. This was granted, with not only ten acres of land on which to build a church and a house, but also a request that his own children might attend the proposed school.

From Bulawayo Mr Radasi took the train to Bembesi Siding. Nearby was the Fingo location, and Chief John Hlazo welcomed him into his home while his own house was built. The Hlazo family had come from the Transkei and it transpired that they knew some of Mr Radasi's people. From Bembesi an eight-mile walk took him to the site allocated, where he lost no time in erecting a little two-roomed wooden house and soon had a square thatched church ready for occupation. Ingwenya Mission had arrived.

First impressions were recorded to friends in Scotland: "This country is full of big forests, and there are still lions, wolves and wild dogs roaming about. Last year the lions came so near Bulawayo that they ate some donkeys about four miles away. It's all thick forest round Bulawayo and you cannot see the town at a distance until you come right up to it." He went on to say that the people "in this part of the country are uncivilised and wear very little clothing, little children no clothing at all. The Matabele live in small two-roomed mud huts with fire made in the middle, no beds but mats to sleep on; no chairs; you have to sit on a mat on the floor. They don't live in the town but are placed in locations. Of course, in Bulawayo and district there are about 6500 Europeans."

That first year there was a drought so severe that the oldest people could not remember ever having experienced anything like it. "The horses and cattle here don't live; they die", wrote Mr Radasi in February. And again in September, "We have not had a drop of rain for seven full months and all the small rivers that are close by have dried up. The only rivers that have not dried up are six miles away and so some of the people here have to walk six miles to get drinking and cooking water from the big rivers that never dry, but some of these are dangerous, as they have crocodiles."

In 1806 he married Annie, a daughter of Chief Hlazo; they named their little daughter Mabel. Mrs Radasi died after a short illness in 1910. In 1915 he married Julia, a daughter of Chief Garner Sojini, and they had a daughter Mildred, and four sons, the youngest of whom was named Edwin.

Few came to hear Mr Radasi at first, but gradually numbers built up. Although some parts of Matabeleland had been visited by missionaries, none of the people around Ingwenya had been influenced by Christianity. From the Fingo location in 1907 a group of men came to the minister desiring to join his congregation. They belonged to the African Presbyterian Church and were among those who had come to Rhodesia as a result of Rhodes' invitation. They had been granted land to which, 100 years later, their descendants would still hold the title deeds. In June 1907 Mr Radasi wrote, "I explained to them our simple mode of worship, which we think is according to Scripture, and that we expected that all who wish to join our Church must submit to all the doctrine and standards of our Church and simple mode of worship, and use only the Psalms of David and no hymns or organs, and that they were not to bring the customs of their churches into ours; and if at any time, even after they had joined us, any of them should think they are not in full sympathy with our doctrine and mode of worship, it would be advisable for those to leave us. I told them that we believed in the whole Bible, from Genesis to Revelation, as the inspired Word of God and accept the whole of the [*Westminster*] *Confession of Faith* as our doctrine and standard. . . . They accepted everything I said."

Some of these men proved most helpful to him, preaching and evangelising in outlying areas. He too travelled extensively, at first on foot or on bicycle before graduating to mule and Scotch cart. Wherever a group of converts was gathered, he opened a preaching station and sometimes also a school after the pattern in Ingwenya – both school and church being conducted under a tree or, during inclement weather, in a little pole-and-dagga thatched building. The sole academic qualification required for teaching in a kraal school was the ability to read.

As a trained singer who enjoyed teaching his congregation to sing in four parts, Mr Radasi demanded a high standard. There were at first only a few metrical psalms in Xhosa; so he was delighted when a booklet of 24 psalms was published, and even more so when the whole psalter became available in 1922. He taught the Scottish psalm tunes – Crimond, Covenanters, Kilmarnock and others – and found the custom of "putting out the line" most useful for teaching the words.

In 1913 the little square church succumbed to the ravages of termites. A larger building was needed in any case; so a more substantial, corrugated iron structure was erected, "a brick-lined building with a stone foundation, ceiled and floored, with an ant-hill

The brick-lined, corrugated iron church at Ingwenya, built in 1913.

A HEART FOR AFRICA

course on the foundation to protect the building from the white ants, which destroy the woodwork". The people contributed maize, goats – whatever they had – to help with costs.

Since his wish was to influence the Matabele to be "people of the Book" Mr Radasi had, from the beginning of his ministry, been teaching them to read. He conducted an evening class for men and soon was running a school for the children. He rewarded achievement with a Bible, which they could then read to their people at home. Teaching was thus a part of his missionary strategy. "Our main object in keeping a school," he wrote, "is that the people may learn to read their Bible, for it is there that they can learn the doctrine of ruin by the Fall, redemption by the blood of Christ and regeneration by the Holy Ghost. These are doctrines absolutely necessary to be taught to the heathen for salvation. . . . Pray for me that I may be faithful in declaring the whole counsel of God and look only to the power and grace of God for success in my labours."

The fame of the school spread, so that pupils came from afar. Most were responsible for their own keep. Some stayed with relatives, while others built temporary accommodation for themselves near the Mission. Some few stayed with Mr Radasi in a private capacity and at his expense. Among these were the sons of Chief Sojini. He was the first Fingo to join the church and conducted services at his own kraal 100 miles east of Ingwenya.

To Paul Hlazo, a nephew of his first wife, Mr Radasi used to say, "One day white people will come here, and there will be a big school at Ingwenya!" And Paul and the other little fellows would look at one another and laugh uproariously.

"Oh yes, you'll see!"

In 1921, when Rev Neil Cameron visited the Mission, 120 pupils were receiving two hours' elementary education daily – Scripture, reading, English and geography. When a pupil had attained a sufficient level of reading ability, he might go on to teach in a kraal school, while a few went on to other missions for further training. The annual government grant for the school was £30 – in total, not per pupil! In the early days of the Mission, parents argued that their children should be paid to come to school – there were better ways of spending their time, and who was to herd the cattle?

Two areas had been allocated to the Matabele for their exclusive use – along the Gwaai and Shangani rivers, forested country less fertile than the central plateau. Ingwenya Mission was situated near the edge of the Ntabazinduna Reserve. By 1923 the reserve was becoming overstocked with cattle so Chief Betisane was moved with some of his people 80 miles north-west to the Shangani Reserve, a thickly forested area criss-crossed by rough footpaths. It was infested by mosquitoes and was a haunt of leopards, lions, elephants, wild dogs and hyenas, to name a few of the animals which roamed at will. The people were largely untouched by civilisation. The chief sent a message to Mr Radasi pleading with him to send a preacher and teacher to Nkayi, where he had settled. John Mpofu and his son Alexander, a teacher, volunteered. They met with bitter opposition but, though tempted to give up, they persevered. It was to prove a significant development in the work of the Mission.

By 1924 Mr Radasi was looking forward to the arrival of a young minister from Scotland to help in the work. Rev John Tallach was due to arrive on 6 November and the event was eagerly anticipated. The people gladly and expectantly built two huts and a kitchen for him and on 4 November Mr Radasi set off for Bembesi Siding, where he was to catch the train for Bulawayo.

Bembesi Siding, where Rev J B Radasi was killed. In the middle is Mr S Nxusani.

A HEART FOR AFRICA

At Bembesi there is no platform. He arrived shortly before his train was due in, on the far side of the tracks. As there was already a train at the station, he crossed in front of it and was walking between the two sets of lines when his train steamed in. He was pulled under the wheels and died instantly.

It now became Stephen Hlazo's sad duty to meet Mr Tallach at Bulawayo. By this time a deacon in the church that Mr Radasi had founded, his mind must have gone back to his first sight of him at that very station almost 20 years earlier. As Mr Tallach emerged from the train, Stephen and a policeman stepped forward to greet him with the shock news.

Rev John Tallach's first duty, then, was to conduct the funeral of the one he had expected to introduce him to his lifework. The whole service spoke of the love of the people for their pastor and the respect with which he was regarded by the whole district and beyond. Mr Tallach wrote that it was evident that their sorrow was "mingled with an intelligent joy, in the belief that all was well with their pastor". On the Lord's Day he preached the usual three services to a large and attentive congregation with Stephen Hlazo interpreting.

Tributes poured in from all over the country, and in Scotland Rev Neil Cameron said, "He was endowed beyond many with wisdom, humility, self-denial and trustworthiness. His faith in the absolute inerrancy and infallibility of the Bible, together with entire dependence on the Holy Spirit . . . was the secret of his success." He was buried at Ingwenya near the church which he had served so wholeheartedly.

The grave of the Rev J B Radasi at Ingwenya.

● CHAPTER 5 ●

The Work Grows

As far back as 1917 Rev N Cameron had been urging praying people to ask the Lord to raise up a young man who might go out to help the work in Africa. He had also urged Mr Radasi to send "a young godly man" home to be educated for the work of the ministry.

Rev John Tallach was born in 1890 in Dornoch on the north-east coast of Scotland, the son of a merchant who was also a lay preacher. After serving in the First World War he offered himself for the Mission field. He qualified in Arts and Divinity and took a course in tropical medicine before sailing for Africa. Some months later Annie Sinclair from Glasgow arrived to be his wife.

He had an uphill struggle for acceptance at first. The people had loved Mr Radasi and had willingly listened to him. He was one of their own and they trusted him – but to listen to a white man? And his coming had coincided with their pastor's

The Rev John Tallach, who laboured for 24 years on the mission field in Africa.

death. He had need of wisdom and all the tact he could muster but with characteristic energy he threw himself into the work.

At first he preached in English, with Paul Hlazo interpreting. He later confessed to being very sceptical as to the effectiveness of an interpreted sermon and recollected how pleased he was when at length people came forward for membership and told how a sermon was blessed to them through Paul's interpretation.

As he was introduced to those villages which had preaching stations, he saw many evidences of a heathen way of life. The religion of the Matabele was a form of animism and it governed many aspects of their lives. They believed in Nkulunkulu, the Great Great One, who concerned himself with rain, famine, war and natural events, but was not at all interested in their personal lives. So great was he that he could not be approached directly but through the amadlosi, the spirits of the ancestors, who in turn were approached through a medium. There were tribal spirits and family spirits whose function was to guard the tribe or family, and care must be taken not to offend them – the ways of doing so being legion. Charms were worn to keep evil spirits at bay. Loyalty to the tribe was paramount. To lie or steal or even to kill was not considered wrong unless against one's own people.

On his journeys, it soon became clear that to visit the kraals with any regularity Mr Tallach would need a car. He bought a second-hand one at his own expense, was shown how to start it up and off he went – no driving test! He did not have enough money to buy petrol; so it just sat at Ingwenya awaiting better times. The Nkayi elders were annoyed that he would not come to visit them. They had heard all about the car, so why was he not coming to Shangani? What was this about petrol? What did petrol matter? When the missionary did get petrol, he and Mrs Tallach bravely set off for Shangani. As a foretaste of things to come, the car came to a standstill – a broken axle. So there they were stranded in the bush till help arrived.

Mr Tallach found that more and more of his time was being spent attending to people in need of medical care. It was becoming obvious that this aspect of his work would be better undertaken by someone with medical training. In 1928 he was relieved of his medical responsibilities by the arrival of Rev Roderick MacDonald, a

The Rev Roderick MacDonald, who served the mission in Africa for 20 years from 1928 to 1948.

native of Applecross on the west coast of Ross-shire. He had graduated in medicine at Edinburgh University and was considering missionary work when he decided to attend the Church's meeting of Synod in Inverness in May 1928. He had been under the impression that there was no place for a doctor at the Mission but now he heard that a doctor was just what was required. He took a course in tropical medicine in London, was ordained on 14 August and sailed out in September. Subsequently Flora Matheson from Glasgow joined him, Mr Tallach performing the marriage ceremony.

Thus began the medical work of the Mission. Soon Dr MacDonald had built a little two-roomed hospital, one room the dispensary, the other a ward with two beds. Floors were of concrete and the roof of corrugated iron. Later on he built two round huts with two beds in each. A small kitchen and stove stood alongside for the use of the patients' relatives; the provision of food was their responsibility. These were the hospital buildings from which Dr MacDonald worked all the years he was at Ingwenya. He was an untrained but gifted carpenter and made all the hospital furniture – a medicine cupboard, instrument cupboard, examination couch, desk and chairs, dentist's chair – whatever was necessary.

A steady stream of out-patients visited the dispensary. In his first year he had 2000 consultations and eventually they numbered 4000 a year. The main complaints were malnutrition, skin diseases, pneumonia and eye trouble as well as burns and minor injuries. Tooth extractions were also carried out. At first the sick were reluctant to become in-patients, but in time the people were to see the benefits of a hospital stay. There was high infant mortality, much of it due to lack of knowledge of hygiene; so he ran a women's class where he gave talks on health care.

A HEART FOR AFRICA

He trained Mr Radasi's eldest daughter Mabel in the basics of first aid and some elementary nursing procedures; so she was able to help in the dispensary, and also visited the sick in their homes; she either cycled or walked, depending on the state of the track. When Mabel later became a teacher, her place was taken by Rhoda Stinta. They were both very conscientious and efficient. As well as home visits Doctor, as everyone called him, held clinics at out-stations, cantering along on horseback in the early years.

The heathen's first recourse when ill was to the witchdoctor. Although witchcraft had been outlawed by the British government since 1903 and some of its more reprehensible features had fallen out of use, it remained the pervasive background to the Africans' thinking, a powerful force that influenced their lives at every turn. Misfortune, illness and death, or even something as mundane as toothache, were attributed to the malice of enemies, or offence caused to the spirits of the ancestors, and it was to the witchdoctor the people turned for enlightenment.

Resplendent in leopard-skin, with monkey tails and feathered headgear, a string of eagles' claws and beads jangling about his neck, he cuts an impressive figure, and to a helpless sufferer in times of ignorance he offered some hope. The sufferer may have walked many miles to consult him. He throws his bones, chants the magic words and studies the resulting pattern. "Ah yes; it's Alamo who has bewitched you. Take this. Payment, two hens." And off the patient goes with a potion that will neutralise the spell. Or he may have offended the amadlosi and must try to win back their favour by holding a feast at which the spirits are given due honour. Or he may be told he has an evil spirit and gashes are then made in his skin to let it escape. Perhaps he is very ill, in which case the probability of his death has to be faced and his grave dug in readiness. If he recovers, a mouse is killed and dropped into the grave and he is free to seek revenge on the culprit.

Dr MacDonald spoke of their "pathetic helplessness" in face of death. What happened, they wondered, to the dead? They believed that the spirit lives on and is able to influence the lives of those left behind. Death was the catalyst for a series of ceremonies that varied according to the status of the deceased: the roots of a certain bush were infused in water which the relatives then drank to banish from their hearts the fear awakened by death. After a fixed interval the tools used in burial were ceremonially washed.

One year later the ceremony of umbuyiso took place, when the spirit of the departed one was welcomed back with drumming and dancing, fighting and feasting, as beer flowed freely. Some was set aside for the deceased one who now had his last chance as an ordinary spirit to give a message to the family. After umbuyiso he became an idlozi and joined the ranks of the guardian spirits of the tribe.

The ceremony of uku-thethela was held in order to appease the ancestral spirits, so that they would not send illness or misfortune. A feast was arranged, again with food and beer in plentiful supply. Relatives were invited and the headman addressed the spirits, telling them that this feast was in their honour so would they take note and please not visit misfortune upon the family? Feasting and jollity followed with dancing and clapping of hands to the wild beat of the drum.

Seedtime and harvest had their rituals. Before the ploughing season began a medicine-man was approached. He had special herbs which were mixed with the seed before planting in order to ensure a good harvest and people would walk miles to obtain this "medicine". In time of drought the rainmaker or diviner came into his own as he proffered advice at a price: try cutting down all trees struck by lightning; search out and destroy all the hawks' nests.

There was the tyranny of superstition; a coiled snake was a sure sign of imminent rain; sticks caught in the branches of trees when the boys were playing might be to blame for the current drought; if milk boiled over it meant the cow would get sick; a garment with even one red thread must not be worn during a thunderstorm. And so they went on grasping at possible explanations for the happenstance of life.

So were their lives darkened and troubled by fears, uncertainty and all kinds of imaginings and suspicions. It took considerable courage and determination to break with these rites and superstitions. Some who came to the clinic visited the witch-doctor as well – just to make sure! In one case the patient was sent home by the witchdoctor with the advice to sit, blanket over head, and inhale the smoke from the fire – which treatment tragically resulted in his death.

There was much need for preaching and teaching, in both of which the two ministers took part for, like Mr Radasi, they saw education as an essential part of their ministry. By the time Mr Tallach had arrived in 1924 about 360 pupils were being taught under the aegis of Ingwenya Mission, 120 at Ingwenya school, the rest in four kraal schools. The policy was that, when there were converts in a village and a preaching station had been established, only then would a school be opened. These schools were at first taught by persons who had simply learned to read and their function was chiefly to teach Bible knowledge and reading. Writing and simple arithmetic were also taught according to the teacher's ability, and cleanliness and order were promoted. The schools were thus an extension of the Mission work of spreading the gospel. Such schools came to be officially designated Kraal Schools – that is, elementary schools taught by an unqualified teacher.

Ingwenya School was classed as a Kraal School because, although Mr Radasi had been a fully-trained teacher he was not employed as such, his primary calling being that of a minister of the Church.

Mr Tallach carried on the work, supervising the schools and teaching as necessary just as Mr Radasi had done. The education offered was a great advance on no education, but it had its limitations. For one thing, Kraal Schools attracted minimum grants, so scope for improvement was limited. Also those pupils wishing to advance beyond the very elementary education received in these schools had to go to other institutions and thus were lost to Ingwenya. Some few pupils were sent, at Mission expense if necessary, to Lovedale in South Africa for a three-year course leading to a teaching certificate; Paul Hlazo had received his further education at St Matthew's Mission and Lovedale and began teaching at Ingwenya in 1925. It was desirable that Ingwenya should take its pupils beyond the elementary stage of education.

This is what Mr Tallach decided to do – Ingwenya School would offer industrial and domestic education, and the elementary education would be extended. A year before his death, Mr Radasi had built a two-roomed school and a small room for domestic work was

Mr Paul Hlazo with a class of pupils at Ingwenya in the early 1940s.

now added. "In addition to the stove etc, we have added six forms, a map of Africa, a blackboard, and arithmetic books for all classes. The large room has been walled off, and sleeping quarters for the girls made of one part of it. I have not yet got a kitchen made for them to cook their own food in but hope to get this done this year."

Paul Hlazo and Miss B Myati were both qualified teachers and very capable. Being qualified, they were due a higher salary and a third teacher, not certificated, was also required. But where was the money to come from? If the school could be upgraded to what became known as a Central School, it would command a more generous grant. But for that to happen, a qualified or an approved European teacher would have to be in charge. Mrs Tallach was not a qualified teacher but she was approved and valiantly stepped in, undertaking the work without salary. Thus the school was in 1927 upgraded from a Kraal to a Central school with four teachers – three African and one European. It attracted about three times the former grant with the great bonus of being able to train its own teachers for the side schools instead of sending them to other institutions for training.

Throughout the years there had been girls in school, but they were greatly outnumbered by the boys. The prevailing view was that girls did not matter. Mr Tallach had other ideas. He was something of a pioneer in his attitude to the education of girls; they were the mothers of the future, he argued, and the well-being of a family was largely in their hands. Girls did matter.

At the opening of the new session Mr Tallach announced that, on an experimental basis, he was willing to take in girls from out-stations, provided their parents undertook to provide their food – so fees were fixed at a bag of mealies and a goat per annum! He would restrict numbers to 20 to see how things would go.

That first year of Ingwenya Central School 24 girls from the outstations were staying on the Mission. The girls from Shangani stayed full time but those from nearer kraals went home for the weekends. In addition another 40 or 50 youngsters attended as day pupils for domestic and industrial instruction. Among the boarders that first year was Esther Donsa, a grand-daughter of Lobengula; her grandmother, MaMlotshwa, was a member in the church.

The new venture was a great success and numbers increased steadily. For the girls it was mind-stretching; it introduced a welcome variety into their lives and gave them a sense of achievement. They learned sewing, basket-making, laundry, cookery and housekeeping – and the parents reaped the benefit.

The boys were not neglected. It was proposed to start agricultural work with them. The Government was approached for an extension of the grounds allocated to the Mission and they were enlarged from 20 to 60 acres. The boys were encouraged to plant vegetables and were allowed to take their produce home – tomatoes, carrots, perhaps egg-plant – their families' appreciation nurturing their enthusiasm.

Wherever necessary, the wives of the missionaries helped in the work of the Mission in an unofficial capacity. Mrs Tallach taught cookery and housekeeping while Mrs Macdonald and Mrs Radasi ran a Bible class for women and encouraged them to bring along their heathen neighbours. The Schools Inspectors spoke of the results, both at Ingwenya and in the kraal schools, as "excellent, wonderful" and the African teachers' houses as among "the cleanest and best" in the circuit.

Soon Mr Tallach was pointing out the need for more staff: "At present there are three chiefs pleading with us to begin work among their people. The population in two of these places is very large. So far we have had to give these places a sorrowful refusal. . . . It is our prayer here that the Lord will put it into the heart of some Christian teacher to undertake the responsibility of the school work. This would leave us free to look after these untouched portions of the field."

In 1928 African education came under the newly-created Department of Native Education, with its own Director and three Inspectors. Subsequently the Department announced that all Central schools would require to have a qualified European teacher in charge – in other words Mrs Tallach would no longer suffice for Ingwenya School. The Department meantime agreed to maintain its status till a suitably qualified teacher should arrive. If no teacher was forthcoming, the school would revert to Kraal status, with consequent loss of grant and all that this would entail.

In August 1932 Mr Tallach informed the home Committee of this requirement, adding that, according to the Native Development Act, the Government would only recognise for grant purposes a teacher either of Industrial subjects or of Domestic Science. However, even if a teacher of Industrial subjects were available, the expense of buying the necessary materials would be prohibitive. Thus it was that the *Free Presbyterian Magazine* of December 1932 carried an appeal for "a teacher who has her certificates in ordinary teaching and Domestic Science".

In June 1932 Mr Tallach and his family left for Scotland sailing from Cape Town on the Edinburgh Castle. His health demanded a change, said Dr Macdonald, after almost eight strenuous years in the field. Edwin Radasi, a teenage son of Mr Radasi, followed some weeks later; his mother had requested Rev Neil Cameron, during his visit to the Mission, that he might be educated in Scotland.

During his furlough Mr Tallach addressed many congregations eager to have first-hand news, and invited questions. He made this comment: "Sometimes it is said that we are making too much of school work. . . . It is the duty of the Church to make use of education as a handmaid to help the gospel. It is our definite thought and feeling on the matter that education is secondary to the gospel."

He was delighted to hear that Jean's offer of service had been gladly accepted.

● Chapter 6 ●

Ingwenya Boarding School

On a bright June day in 1933 Jean and her mother set off for Africa. Since Mackinlay was pursuing his career at sea, Mrs Nicolson had decided to pack up and go with Jean; while Jean devoted herself to teaching, she would be responsible for looking after the home. Travelling with them was the Tallach family, now returning after their first leave.

After a fortnight's sailing they berthed at Cape Town, with its spectacular backdrop of Table Mountain, so often covered with white mist. The Nicolsons spent three weeks there visiting Mrs Nicolson's sister Barbara and her family before embarking on the three-day train journey through Cape Province and the Hex River Valley, with its wonderful orchards and vineyards, on to Kimberley and Mafeking with their evocative overtones, over sun-bleached grassland and finally up, up to the high veldt till they finally pulled in at Bulawayo. At stops en route the train was besieged by poorly-clad adults and children, begging for pennies and left-over scraps of food – a disturbing experience, pointing up as it did the inequalities and injustices on a planet of plenty.

At Bulawayo Rev John Tallach met them and they set off in the Mission car in a northerly direction on the Salisbury road. For the first 24 miles the road was, at that time and for many years to come, a dirt road with two useful tarred strips for the wheels to race over. The

Above: Group on board ship in 1933 to see Rev John Tallach, Mrs Tallach and their children off, returning from furlough, and Miss Jean Nicolson and her mother going out to Africa for the first time. Left to right: Miss Graham, Jean Nicolson, Rev J P MacQueen, Mrs Nicolson, Rev John Tallach, Robert Sinclair (elder, London), Ida Tallach, Annie Tallach, Catherine and James Tallach. Below: Mrs Annie Tallach and children, Catherine and James, pictured with Jean (left) and Mrs Nicolson (right).

A HEART FOR AFRICA

next stretch was different. A track veered off to the left through the veldt and, for the next six miles, the car rattled and jolted over ruts, and into dips and dry river-beds, swung round trees and passed kraals with firelight flickering through open doorways. They topped a rise and suddenly they were at Ingwenya. There they received the warmest of welcomes from the Tallach and Macdonald families, who were immensely cheered and uplifted by this addition to the company. Till their own house was completed, the Nicolsons were to enjoy the hospitality of the Tallach family, happily settled into their new house built a few years previously.

Ingwenya, in the Ntabazinduna Reserve, is on an extended plateau as high above sea level as Ben Nevis, Scotland's highest mountain. So, though only 20 degrees south of the equator, it enjoys a pleasant and healthy climate. Thorn bushes dot the dry and tawny veldt under wide skies giving a feeling of endless space. A few large trees here and there were all that remained of the forest that had once sheltered abundant wildlife; otherwise all was bare scrub. In the Mission compound grew handsome trees laden with blossom – jacaranda and flamboyant – which gave welcome shade. There were

A contemporary picture of some of the many jacaranda trees in blossom at Ingweyna.

the teachers' little mud-brick houses, the hospital, the school, the boarders' huts, the two small corrugated iron huts with thatched roof occupied by the Macdonald family and, in the middle of the compound, the church – simple little buildings perhaps, but clear evidence of what had been accomplished and hints of what might yet be. Goats and hens wandered about poking nosily here and there.

And the people – always Jean's first interest! The newcomers found themselves among a friendly, courteous people with delightful manners. Soon they had learned how to respond to the customary greeting as the women, curious little heads peeping shyly from behind their skirts, shook hands with a slight curtsey and a polite "Salibonani".

"Yebo. Linjani?"

"Sikhona."

The new headmistress and her mother were scrutinised with interest. Twenty-five year old Jean was tall and slim with an erect, dignified carriage which she kept till the end of her life. Mrs Nicolson with her commanding presence was more forceful than her daughter. Together they must have made quite an impact on arriving at the Mission, and they certainly did in the long term – but that lay in the future.

Jean had come to teach and she threw herself straight into the work of the new term. Since it was the last term she fitted in to the current routine, leaving any changes till the new session, which would start in January. The school was the same two-room mud-brick building with thatched roof built by Mr Radasi. Jean taught in one room and Paul Hlazo in the other, while Mabel Radasi taught in the church. Sometimes a class was held outside under a tree. Since the dormitory could not house all 50 girl boarders – there were no boy boarders in those days – one of the classrooms doubled up as sleeping quarters. In the morning the girls rolled up their mats and blankets and stacked them in a corner.

There were eight stages in the school: Sub-A and Sub-B were followed by Standards 1 to 6, the final year being equivalent to the level reached by the end of primary school in Scotland. Pupils started school at any age whatever, so any class might have pupils of various ages depending on how old they were on starting school and how quickly they had progressed. Jean taught the upper three Standards. Some of the girls were a mere two or three years younger than she! Some, of course, did not know how old they were.

As she looked at the eager young faces before her, she thought, "They all look the same!" But it was not long before she decided that her pupils were as different in looks and personality as were the children back home in Scotland. As for putting names to faces! There were Ndebele names like Sibonisiwe, Biblical names, English names – and others. A mother might like the crisp sound of "sixpence" and so her new baby was Sixpence! Jean found some of the names amusing at first – there was a Matches and a smiling Lizard – but the strange thing was that in no time at all the personality of the child took over and obliterated the seeming incongruity of the name.

These early days remained fresh in her memory. "These were days of great drought. There had been no rain for months. We had a very poor fence round the Mission, and goats and donkeys used to wander around looking for water. The goats were so mad with thirst that they would force their way into the class-rooms and dive under the desks searching for water – there were no doors, no panes in the windows. A hen used to come into the class-room and lay an egg nearly every day. This interested me very much as I had been brought up in a large city where such things do not happen!"

The beginners wrote on slates, sometimes balancing them on their knees as best they could when pupil numbers exceeded desks. Mr Tallach described how cheerfully the new headmistress faced difficulties; "No decent schoolrooms, no glass in the windows but just big holes in walls and the dust coming in, no place to get warm in the winter time, every place cramped, desks home-made. I went down one time to the store and asked how many boxes I could get – we get 4-gallon tins of paraffin in a wooden box and they sell the wooden boxes cheap, at one shilling each. I remember I went down to the storeman one day and bought two dozen of these. I took them home, put them together and made desks of them and put legs on them. I had them there and was afraid to show them to anybody. I knew some people would laugh at them and, above all, I was afraid to show them to Miss Nicolson! I could not introduce to a teacher from a well-equipped school in Scotland these boxes that her pupils would have to use as best they could. However, I introduced Miss Nicolson to the desks and she said, 'They will do fine', and that was the spirit all through. Miss Nicolson recognised, like myself, that we had not a great amount of money to draw on but we were determined to raise the status of the school . . . . It is owing to her that we have a boarding school. It is owing to Mr Radasi that we have a mission."

The children took to her straight away as children do to a young and friendly teacher. Invariably there were offers galore to carry her exercise books and, as they crowded round, she would distribute a small bundle to one and another. One day as she crossed the compound two little girls came running after her: "Misi, can we carry your books?"

"But I have no books today, dear."

"Oh!" Disappointment. Then brightening, "Misi, can we carry your pencil?"

"Thank you!"

Because the school now had a qualified teacher, the boarding department was officially recognised as a Boarding School while the day department retained its status as a Central School. In return for consequent benefits, mainly an increased grant, a higher standard all round was expected. It was a challenge, but things were looking up at what was now known as Ingwenya Boarding School.

The Department's resources were concentrated, almost exclusively, in the lower end of Primary school. As many young people as possible were to receive some education. Most children still did not in fact stay beyond Standard 1. The work of the upper classes was confined to practical subjects which would enable the boys to manage the land better and the girls the home. Education to a higher level was encouraged only so far as it served the needs of the community for teachers, nurses or community workers.

Although education in Africa was usually the preserve of boys – and the roll did include boys – Ingwenya was essentially a girls' school. The usual primary subjects were taught. The pupils learned to speak and read English and Xhosa, the Fingo language, although most of them were Matabele whose language is Ndebele. Few books were printed in Ndebele and the Bibles and Psalm books were in Xhosa; hence the desirability of knowing Xhosa.

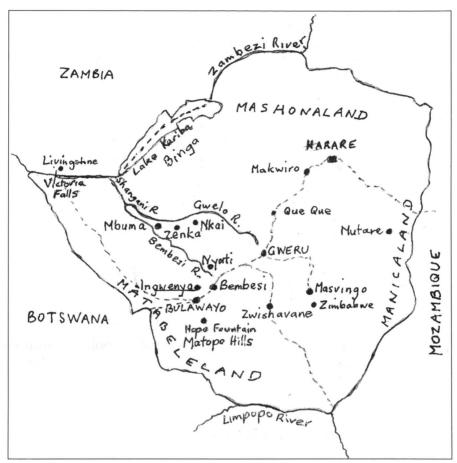

Map of Zimbabwe showing place names mentioned in this book.

Schools were inspected regularly. A Junior school syllabus was supplied by the Government and a suggested time-table drafted for each class, which was to be followed as closely as possible. Each teacher must also have a week-by-week scheme of work and a detailed record of the work done during the year, all of which were closely examined by the Inspector.

The impact of a qualified teacher taking over full-time responsibility for education was felt immediately. The effect on morale was palpable. The teachers gained in confidence, while Mr Tallach, freed from school responsibilities, had time to visit heathen kraals which he did every weekday except Saturday. In his annual report he told the Synod that the local people, "whether adults or children, require some understanding and 'Misi' seems to have understood them immediately. To us it was a wonder to see the trust they immediately placed in her; there seemed to be no suspicion. This I take it is owing to her large sympathy. The school is now run on systematic lines and a new life has entered into all parts of it."

Everyone helped in any way they could. Dr Macdonald taught First Aid and Hygiene. Mr Tallach took Scripture. Mrs Macdonald and Mrs Tallach continued to help with Domestic Science. Inevitably Mrs Nicolson was roped in. On Wednesdays she held a women's needlework class and also taught in the school.

The new session began at the end of January 1934 with 150 pupils, 40 of them boys, and three teachers, one of whom was Mabel Radasi and another Paul Hlazo – he who had laughed at the very idea of white people coming to Ingwenya! For the first time it had a Standard 6. As far as possible the latest methods were used in teaching. In English, for example, they used readers printed in South Africa rather than those from overseas because, though expensive,

Group of teachers and children with Mrs Mabel Radasi (seated) – the widow of Rev John Radasi.

A HEART FOR AFRICA

their vocabulary was familiar; as Jean pointed out, "In this part of the country there are neither hills, lakes, forests, permanent rivers, bridges, sea or ships."

Each day began with half an hour of Bible teaching. In fact more time was allocated to Scripture than to any other single subject on the curriculum. With the older students Jean sometimes read more unfamiliar parts of the Bible. One chapter she liked to discuss with them was Micah 7 and especially the verses, "Rejoice not against me, O mine enemy: when I fall, I shall arise; when I sit in darkness, the Lord shall be a light unto me. I will bear the indignation of the Lord, because I have sinned against Him, until He plead my cause, and execute judgment for me: He will bring me forth to the light, and I shall behold His righteousness." She would tell them about Captain K K Macleod and how, as he lay injured on the battlefield, these words came into his mind and gave him great encouragement.

Another story she liked to tell was about a missionary who went to a people who had never heard the gospel and preached month after month with no apparent success. He had started at Genesis and worked his way through the Old Testament and, no matter how he exhorted them, they remained impassive. Then he moved on to the New Testament and, when he told them about Jesus and how He had died for sinners, they asked, "Why didn't you tell us before?" So she would help these young people to appreciate and memorise parts of Scripture.

As the boys had to go off herding cattle at 11 am the academic subjects – the three R's and such – were taught from 7.30 am till 10.30 am, when there was a short break. The girls then had two hours of domestic work after which the 60 day-girls went home. In the afternoon the boarders did Industrial work. After the boys had gone, the girls settled down to one or another of the Domestic subjects – housekeeping, cookery, laundry or hygiene. The ultimate aim was to have the girls put into practice in their own homes what they learned in these classes. Education was to be as natural and near to their home life as possible.

For a lesson in African housekeeping, a teacher would set off with her class to a neighbouring kraal – previously alerted, of course. There they would do a thorough "spring clean" – hang out skins and blankets to air, wash pots, sweep the floor and smear it with manure. The yard was then tackled. In time Jean thought, So much walking to and fro! Why not clean and polish the floors in the classrooms? – and there were desks that could do with a scrubbing. So that became the rule – a learning-by-doing where need arose.

For European housework, the ladies on the Mission allowed their houses to be used for demonstration purposes, under supervision. Many of the children had never been inside a European home and were understandably much more interested in looking around than in listening to their teacher. Despite her best efforts, little groups of girls would gather here and there giggling at their reflection in a mirror, examining ornaments, gasping at the shelves of books or exclaiming at the chiming of a clock. The windows were a constant delight, for their homes had neither doors nor glazed windows and they would stand gazing out at the view.

European housework had the excitement of novelty. Bed-making was a favourite lesson; very few of them had ever seen a bed and they learned so much more than merely how to make a bed: they acquired a vocabulary; they heard, for instance, that the wool for the blankets came from sheep. This idea intrigued them for the sheep they knew had very little wool, were in fact hardly distinguishable from goats, and were never sheared. Aware that the pupils probably slept with their heads under the blankets the headmistress stressed, "It is most important to keep your head out from under the blankets, most important. Fresh air . . . ." The girls thought of spiders, mosquitoes, rats and snakes and kept their counsel!

Setting the table was fun. At home people generally sat on the floor and used their hands to eat out of a common pot or basin. Now they had to arrange this strange conglomeration of implements just so. The next step was learning table manners, so the girls took it in turns to sit at table and grapple with knife and fork to much hilarity from the onlookers.

In Cookery they used such utensils as might be found in their own homes – a tin basin or two, an iron spoon, an iron cooking pot – so that the gulf to be bridged between school and home would not be too great. Cooking was done outdoors on a fire of twigs. An attempt was made to induce the girls and, through them, their mothers to make use of eggs, milk and chicken as they had a prejudice against these foods. They tried various ways of cooking eggs and, after learning about the food value of milk, they made butter and cheese. Substitutes were suggested for the ingredients used in European recipes; honey could be used in place of sugar and monkey-nut oil in place of butter. With mealie meal – flour made from maize – they baked bread and scones, using their own home-made yeast known as amarewa.

Dr Macdonald very much approved of all this teaching: "Direct medical intervention can avail little where the root cause of the trouble is lack of proper food". He described the people's diet as "terribly monotonous. Maize meal and millet, the former especially of a kind particularly deficient in vitamins, is the staple diet. Cows' milk and some herbs they may have for a part of the year, but for quite six months all but a few are without green or fresh food of any kind."

Laundry the girls disliked. It was hard work and fraught with frustration; walk to the well, await your turn, let down the bucket, wait, haul it up, empty it into your pail, drop a twig or leaf on top to prevent spilling, heave the heavy container on to your head and walk back to the little laundry. And after all that, as Jean remembered, sometimes while she was giving instructions and her back was turned, the goats would drink the water. "So I had to keep my eye on the goats as well as on the children! However, when you are young you do not worry too much."

Doctor taught Hygiene and First Aid. In the beginners' class Hygiene concentrated on the practical. "One day in the week," wrote Jean, "is chosen as head-washing day and all those whose curls are grey with dust are used for demonstration purposes and plunged in a bath of water. Another day is tooth day and a plant is shown, the stem of which makes an excellent brush. Then on slate-washing day there is shown a method of cleaning more hygienic than using the tongue! These children come from kraals within a radius of two or three miles. Some belong to our own people, some to heathen homes."

So the morning was occupied. At 1 pm the day-girls went home hungry, for most had not eaten since the previous evening – in their homes there were commonly two meals a day, the first about noon and the second in the evening. The boarders had a one-hour break. Jean went home laden with exercise-books.

In the afternoon the boarder girls had two hours of industrial work – needlework, basketry, pottery, knitting or child welfare. Needlework enjoyed a high profile. Mrs Macdonald took the sewing classes and Government Inspectors demanded as high a standard as in the well-equipped schools in town. The older girls made their own clothes and proudly wore the pretty dresses made from materials sent from Canada and Scotland. Jean expressed their gratitude in words the girls themselves would use. "To all those ladies who have done so much already we would say, 'Lingadinwa. Don't be tired'. To the few who haven't yet begun we would commend these loveable children, who are often enticed to school by seeing a pretty garment on a neighbouring child, apparently so small a thing bringing them within reach of all those good things which they so often learn to love and treasure.

"The girls take great pleasure in choosing a length of print from the cloth on hand and develop quite a taste for what is fresh, pretty and good-wearing. Even the little girls tip-toe to test the material between finger and thumb and ask in broken English, 'Is it coming out?' meaning, Will the pattern wash out? Their print dresses have to stand a great deal of hard wear. At school the dresses are always washed once a week and when there is an unexpected shower during the rainy season no one can resist having an extra washing day and every available bush around Ingwenya School is hung with drying garments. When, in addition, one remembers the heat of the African sun, the scarcity of soap and that, when too worn and thin for outer use and with patches more in evidence than the original, the print dress becomes an undergarment, it can be seen how much appreciated good prints are!" Nothing was wasted. All scraps and oddments were gratefully received at the Friday Patching Class, where the girls diligently mended their own clothes and those of brothers and sisters – if the patch matched, it was a bonus.

The older girls followed a higher course in needlework, including hem-stitching, crochet, embroidery and beadwork. This they much preferred to pottery and basketry and proved to have an aptitude for it. As a people they were gifted in music and art and those with an artistic bent produced beautiful work and were able to earn welcome cash – though less than their work was worth – by selling tray cloths, tablecloths or bedspreads. Thus they could buy such luxuries as soap, scissors, needles and thread.

Most of the material used in the basketry class was found in the neighbourhood. The baskets they made were practical rather than ornamental. The clay for pottery was likewise found locally and the articles were fired by the girls themselves. After mastering the shaping and firing, they went on to add decoration using local dyes. With the clay they also made apparatus for use in the lower classes and out-schools: letters and numbers, models of kraals, animals and birds. The teachers were grateful to have these for such activities as counting, reading and language. But the most popular class of all was the knitting class; "The girls think it a great triumph to take home a pair of socks for father or brother, a present much appreciated by the menfolk and a more convincing argument than any other that it pays to educate the girls!"

One afternoon, as Jean was teaching, she became aware of a restless and suppressed impatience among the girls. Locusts! Swarms of the destructive insects were not uncommon in the early years of the Mission. They could arrive like a black cloud and devour every green blade in sight. On the other hand they were a tasty addition to the diet and the girls were itching to get to them. As soon as released from captivity they were out among the crowd scooping them up in their aprons, for a swarm had landed in the bush less than a mile away. There was a harvest jollity as loads of the delicacy were carted off to be roasted or dried.

They were a happy company despite having little leisure time. In late afternoon, while some sat sunning themselves outside their dormitories with crochet or knitting, the girls whose turn it was to fetch water went back and fore to the well, a joyful errand when it was full. But when the water level was low, they had to be out at dawn to get there before the workers drained it dry, or sit for an hour by the old well near the river waiting in turn with women from the neighbouring kraals.

A group wandered in the fields searching for idelele (okra, a green vegetable) to cook and eat with their evening meal of thick porridge, or gathered wild fruits – plums, apples or olives. They had names for all the plants, and each plant had some reputed or real virtue – perhaps as a remedy for various ills or, like inkunzana, a practical use; it gave a thick lather when placed in water.

Others set to work preparing the main meal of the day. They gathered brushwood to light two or three small fires, the sharp sounds of snapping twigs punctuating their happy chatter. Sometimes Mfundisi (the minister), who took a fatherly interest in them, would come by with isijebo – vegetables or meat to have with their porridge. After supper their songs and laughter carried on the still evening air as they played by the dying light of the embers. Darkness fell rather suddenly between six and seven o'clock with not much variance between summer and winter. As it was early to rise, so it was early to bed.

Friday afternoon was "tidying-up" time. The school was given a thorough clean. The church had to be left ready for the Sabbath services. As they dusted and polished, and swept the pathways with branches the girls sang, "Siyasebenza lo mama; We are working with Mama."

"One Friday," remembered Jean, "as we were busy, a boy came to the school on a bicycle, which we used to call an isigogogo – you can guess why. It was a very hot day. He handed me a large tin and a letter from a teacher in one of the out-schools, Mr Sobantu – Monde's father, then a young man – who said he hoped I would like his present. When I looked into the tin here were two small animals, a bit like dogs with very sharp ears. I did not know what they were. I sent for teacher Paul Hlazo. 'Oh!' he said, 'They are baby jackals! When they grow up, they will eat your mother's hens!' So – we gave them milk, and back they went with a letter of thanks!"

Jean took pleasure in keeping the place spruce and tidy. This was in keeping with her nature and with her conviction that the mission should be a civilising influence in every aspect of its work. Besides, she was a teacher and understood the power of example. She wrote, "Within a certain radius of the Mission most of the kraals are neat and clean. A circular fence of thorn bushes, tightly packed together, surrounds a few round huts and within this enclosure the yard is usually swept and clean. One hut acts as a kitchen where the food is cooked on a fire in the centre of the floor, the smoke issuing from the door .. . . . There are sleeping huts containing skins and blankets, but windows are rarely found. The more advanced kraals have a hut where the family sit at times, and there one may find a box or table with a few plates and cups, a calabash where the milk ferments and, it may be, a barrel half-full of dried locusts."

She was conscious that at Ingwenya they touched only the fringes of local life. "Further afield," she went on, "one comes into contact with real heathen homes and people. With a cattle kraal immediately in front of the dwelling huts, the dirt is indescribable. Children, naked and often covered in sores, sit amid the squalor making no attempt to brush the flies off their faces. Poverty so extreme can hardly be imagined. Nothing in the way of domestic equipment is to be seen with the exception of a clay pot – no plates or spoons; no remnants of cloth, as any garments are made at the local store; not even a sheet of paper."

It was from homes such as these that some of the girls came. Doctor spoke of a girl in her early teens who had come from a heathen kraal to Ingwenya: "No particular notice was taken of her, but she progressed and was learning just like all the others, but later she came forward to be baptised. Now I may mention that when . . . people come forward to be baptised . . . the examination is just the same as if they had come forward asking for full membership of the Church. . . . This girl received baptism, and it transpired later that quietly during her holidays she went home to a heathen kraal and there on her own initiative began family worship and insisted on reading the Bible to her parents."

Kraals might appear disorganised and untidy to the onlooker, but caution was required in judging standards. In spite of scarcity of water and what might look like poor hygiene, disease was not rife. For example, the cattle kraal might appear to be too near the dwellings, but in fact the position would be carefully chosen so that it was downwind of the homes.

The girls came from a variety of social and Church backgrounds – Seventh Day Adventist, Wesleyan, Church of England, American Baptist and others. A few were brought up in truly Christian homes. However, except for the Christian girls, all were, beneath a veneer of civilisation, heathen in their attitude to social and moral questions. But the old order was disintegrating and discipline in the home was often slack.

Jean remarked of the girls that, while different in character and disposition, yet "almost without exception they are docile, loveable and eager to please. The difference between a newcomer and a girl who has been a few years in school is very marked. Some knowledge of English, suitable clothing, a few responsibilities of her own, make the schoolgirl self-confident and resourceful."

And Mr Tallach gladly observed, "So far as the gospel among the school girls is concerned we have to praise the Lord that He has given us great encouragement during the year. Seven older girls were given full privileges and three of the younger ones received the sacrament of baptism . . . some of those members are now teaching the Sabbath School and come to me on Saturdays for Sabbath School lessons."

Jean pictured with a group of girl pupils in the 1930s.

A HEART FOR AFRICA

● CHAPTER 7 ●

Home at Ingwenya

MRS NICOLSON took charge at home. Their house was ready for occupation in December and in no time it was as home-like and attractive as ingenuity and taste could make it. From outside it might be a humble little building but it was a joy to enter.

The ladies had a well-ordered lifestyle. The house was simply furnished but life was conducted in the same genteel manner as Mrs Nicolson had run her home in Scotland. Everything was kept in spotless condition by the girls and lads who worked for them; this was a welcome source of income for the young people and valuable training too. Even the routine of morning and evening family worship, and grace before and after meals, and the orderliness and details of daily living were a form of education.

The stone floors were rubbed to a mirror shine with red polish applied once or twice a week. The tilley lamps were burnished, the wick trimmed and the oil checked. Dust was banished.

At night the tilley lamp hissed and glowed, cosy and friendly, but a magnet to the cloud of swirling insects that appeared from nowhere. The open thatch allowed air to circulate freely -- and the ladies closed their minds to whatever else might also be circulating. Shortly after they moved in they became aware of a persistent humming which was eventually traced to a drawer in a dressing-table. Doctor came to the rescue with a cloth soaked in chloroform

Above: In front of the Nicolsons' house in the 1930s. Back row, left to right: Rev John Tallach, Jean Nicolson, Dr MacDonald holding Alasdair. Front row: Miss Johann MacAskill, James Tallach, Mrs Annie Tallach, Catherine Tallach, Mrs Jessie Nicolson, Mrs Flora MacDonald. Below: MIssion staff in front of the Nicolsons' house in 1935.

A HEART FOR AFRICA

which quickly put the bees to sleep; and they awoke in surroundings that better pleased the Nicolsons.

The ministers' families were a constant source of interest and delight. In time there were five Tallach children – Catherine, James and Ian, who acquired a life-long ability to speak Ndebele fluently, and the twins Helen and Margaret. There were four boys in the Macdonald family – Alasdair, Duncan, Iain and Donald. Their parents undertook their primary education and as they grew older, they graduated to correspondence courses – a lonely and difficult way to learn – while Jean helped out with French.

The European and African children played together chattering happily in Ndebele. When Mrs Nxusani, a fine Christian, came to teach at Ingwenya little Sipho was just the right age for a playmate for Ian and Alasdair. He was full of fun and mischief and became a great favourite with everyone. Games, involving singing, chasing and hand-clapping, were of the simple sort that find a parallel in many cultures.

Having got the inside of the house to rights, Mrs Nicolson turned her attention to making a flower garden. That done she looked around to see where she would plant her trees and soon a curve of young syringa trees led from the gate of the compound to their house – a delight when covered in heads of perfumed lilac.

Hens next! She went to see a farmer in the vicinity, Mr Mackay, from whom she bought first-class hens which became her pride and joy. In the process she and the Mackays, with daughter Joy, became friends whom they invited to the Mission and who in turn entertained them on their vast ranch – European farmers had the best land and invariably prospered accordingly. The Nicolsons made many friends – families in Bulawayo, people they met on their travels, some with whom they had business dealings. Saturdays would occasionally find them entertaining American Baptists from the Matopos Mission or the Masefields of Mohem Mine, a gold-mine no longer being worked.

When guests were expected the table was set with a crisp linen tablecloth and napkins. The crystal glasses shone and the silver table service received by Captain Nicolson from the crew of the *City of Seattle* doubtless made its appearance. The housemaids serving at table wore starched white aprons.

Mrs Nicolson had pretty china and impressed on her young helpers that care must be taken when handling cups and saucers belonging to a set. As for the odd cups – they could be left to their fate. So when Howard appeared in the doorway apologetically holding tell-tale pieces of broken china she was dismayed.

"Not one of our good set!"

"No, Ma'am; she have no brother!"

There were occasional jaunts into town. Mr Tallach was a friendly outgoing man with many acquaintances there and whenever he or Doctor had business to do they would thoughtfully offer the ladies a lift. Jean was very grateful. The rattle-around was worth it for the pleasure of being in the big wide world and no doubt the sight of shops and pavements and the buzz of traffic had an allure for a girl brought up in the city. And it was a change!

Mrs Nicolson had a little one-room guest house built. It stood trim but empty in its strip of garden. One day she received a letter from a Mrs MacIver, originally from Applecross but at that time living in New York. It included a gift of money. Mrs MacIver was a talented artist. She had recently sold some of her paintings and the proceeds

The guest house furnished with a gift from a friend, Mrs MacIver, of Winnipeg and New York. It was in use for many years.

A HEART FOR AFRICA

were for Mrs Nicolson's personal use. A few months later a similar gift was received and so the guest house was furnished. Among the first to enjoy its comfort were Mary Gatherar and her mother. Aunt Johan came too and Mr Tallach wrote, "We looked forward with such pleasure to her visit and our expectation was not disappointed. The smell of the sea and the smell of the heather still lingers about Ingwenya."

When a third gift arrived Mrs Nicolson announced, "The Mission needs a cow; I'm off to see Mr Mackay!" And away she went and came back with a splendid Jersey cow, the Mission's first.

Mrs Nicolson and Jean with Mary Gatherar, from Scotland. Miss Gatherar was a University friend of Jean's – she and her mother visited the Mission in the 1930s.

The school year was the reverse of what Jean had known in Scotland. It began towards the end of January and finished in early December. There was a short holiday in early April and another in early August.

In the dry winter season, approximately June till September, the weather is fresh and pleasantly warm and the landscape takes on what to Scottish eyes looks like an autumn-spring combination as occasional green appears among the tawny shades. It can for brief spells be bitterly cold when the amakaza, a south wind, brings cloud and drizzle and a chilling damp, like a raw Scotch mist. The hot, rainy season begins in November or December. The earth is covered in a shimmer of green and everything comes to life under the transforming effect of the rain. Wild flowers spring up in unexpected places and buds suddenly appear on the trees. This is sowing and planting time. The rainy season lasts till about February. Harvest follows, and the cooler air of autumn. All of which is a very general pattern.

It was in the rainy season that snakes were a hazard – green mambas, black mambas, puff adders and cobras, among others. Mr Tallach reported in one letter that they had recently killed eight snakes of a particularly venomous type. One, six-foot long, had been dispatched the previous day and they had found two in the house – quite a concern with young children around.

Mrs Nicolson waged her own personal vendetta against the serpents. Of an afternoon she might be found sitting on a chair beside a snake-hole for hours on end, sunhat firmly on head, sturdy stick at the ready, calmly knitting with one eye on the hole the other on the sock in her hand. No snake was going to get her hens!

The Nicolsons had arrived in a period of drought. Crops withered; there was no grass; animals died. There had been an outbreak of foot-and-mouth disease among the cattle. The people were hungry, ill-clad, under-nourished; children suffered from scurvy because of the lack of fresh green vegetables. To compound difficulties, the years of the world-wide Depression following the Wall Street crash in 1929 were felt in Rhodesia as elsewhere. There was great poverty. The Church in Scotland sent out money but it was so little in comparison to the need.

When rain fell in plenty that November, there was great rejoicing. The women got to work in the fields, tilling the hard earth and planting the mealies to the rhythm of the songs that turned hard work into fun. Agriculture was their work. It was purely subsistence farming. Each married woman had her own hut and a field where she grew maize and vegetables for her household. Hoeing, sowing, reaping, all this was their responsibility. To save their precious seed they often had to take on the role of scarecrow, sitting beside their fields ready to drive the birds away. Their reward would come when, in May or June, they carried home the harvest in big bundles on their heads. The girls of the family helped; a five-year-old would start with a little load which would grow with the years.

Back at the kraal they ground the mealies into the meal which constituted their staple diet. It was made into a kind of thick porridge which in time of plenty was eaten with vegetables or meat. At meal-times each would help himself to a small ball of porridge and dip it in the stew.

The men helped with work in the fields at weeding-time. Then it was all hands to the task – men, women, children, tiny tots. Such work demanded beer, and plenty of it, and all were free to drink, even children!

Women were the burden-bearers. It was they who fetched water from the well. It was a common sight to see a woman make her way home with a 6-gallon pail on her head, knitting as she went. It was the women who in like fashion carried home firewood – almost hidden under the scrabbled-together load of branches and twigs. They might walk many miles over rough ground, load on head, baby on back and two hands full.

Among the Matabele, women were accorded an inferior status and had few rights. They could make no decisions of their own. Before a woman could receive medical treatment she must have her husband's permission. Doctor found that this was usually given but, if not, nothing could be done. One man flatly refused to let his wife go into hospital. "But she must have this operation. Why are you so much opposed to it?" "Because she's needed to work in the fields!" And that was that! On another occasion Doctor remonstrated with a mother doing her best to look after her baby of five months ill with diarrhoea. No amount of pleading would induce her to seek medical attention for the little one; she must await her husband's return. He was working away from home and would not be back for a month.

The rains were not constant; rather they tended to come in heavy downpours with hot, dry spells between. Twenty minutes of tropical rain could turn any journey into an adventure, of sorts!

One day Mrs Nicolson and Jean borrowed the Mission car to visit friends on a farm some distance away. On their way home in late afternoon they were caught by one of those sudden flash-floods. The rain came down in sheets and, by the time they reached the ford, the normally dry river bed was in full flood with water rushing across their path, which was by then a quagmire. With the river rapidly overspreading its banks, there was nothing they could do but sit in the car as the water level rose around them. Darkness fell and there

Rev James Fraser contemplates a flooded river crossing near Ingwenya.

they were stuck with no means of alerting anyone. It was a long and anxious night. When the sun arose, how welcome its heat and light! The water gradually subsided and, when it was safe to do so, they crossed over, arriving home tired, hungry and thankful for God's safe keeping.

With ever-increasing numbers of girls requesting school places each year it became imperative to build more accommodation; so the two ministers, true Jacks-of-all-trades, set to organising the work and sharing in it themselves. Local children who were turned away could often find a place in a kraal school but it was heartbreaking having to refuse 30 or 40 requests each year for boarding places. It was planned to build six houses and a washroom for the girls as well as accommodation for teachers.

Jean immediately saw the potential for an educational "project" – that is, exploiting the pupils' natural interest in the goings-on at the site to support her teaching. By being involved in the building work they would acquire skills and knowledge. They observed with a view to learning; they made various measurements, calculated the number of bricks needed, described what they saw, and perhaps drew

A HEART FOR AFRICA

diagrams, expanding their vocabulary in the process. The boys witnessed the laying of the foundation, the erection of the walls and made a contribution of small bricks to be used for the interior walls. The girls plastered the walls, outside and in, with clay and with wooden mallets beat the dagga floors to a smooth polished surface. "The provision of grass floor mats, water pots, and curtains will occupy the girls for some time. It is not only that they acquire a skill in these simple furnishings, but many of them will be confronted with a new idea, that of home-making. The African's hut is a shelter where he sleeps at night on a skin or mat. His life is spent out of doors. All the simple arrangements that constitute home-life are absent; for example no one thinks of preparing an early meal for the man who leaves home in the morning, or for the children who go to school."

The sheer luxury of properly designated quarters for the boarders gave everyone a lift. The layout was simple and attractive. Each house, neatly thatched and plastered in grey clay, consisted of two rooms with a little kitchen at the back with a fireplace. They were arranged in two rows facing each other with the teachers' house across one end; it looked down the road which was lined with jacaranda trees, under which bloomed plots of bright geraniums.

Mrs Radasi was appointed boarding mistress and the girls enjoyed choosing a name for their own house. In each house a head-girl was in charge; she was responsible for seeing that all was kept clean and in order. The girls took weekly turns in fetching water, providing food and preparing meals for the resident teachers and themselves. Before school at 7.30 am, all the schoolrooms and dormitories had to be swept and dusted. Sleeping-mats and blankets were neatly rolled up and placed on top of their boxes on the floor. All then met for worship in the church but in the evening each head-girl was responsible for taking family worship in her house.

School was still being held in the little two-roomed hut built by Mr Radasi. Three hundred pupils were being taught by three teachers, each with a composite class of 80 pupils, while Jean was responsible for a smaller class as well as for general supervision. Mrs Tallach and Mrs Macdonald were totally responsible for sewing and domestic subjects. Doctor and Mfundisi helped out wherever necessary. So cramped for space were they that some of Standards 2 and 3 sat on the floor because there was no room for both children and desks. Two teachers taught in the church. Often a class escaped to the shade of a large gum tree!

It need hardly be said that the need for more accommodation was urgent; so now that the boarders were comfortably housed, work began on the school. Jean described it as an attractive building, long and low and neatly thatched, divided into three rooms, each entered through a small porch of its own. The centre room was the smallest, with two larger classrooms on either side. Mr Tallach made wall blackboards of fine sand and clay, while the girls, by now experts, beat the earthen floors and plastered the walls. Various precautions were taken in the form of insecticides to prevent white ants from coming through the walls to destroy blackboards and pictures. A sickroom and the girls' first-ever dining-room were built, also a small hut that the girls called a praying room for the boarders' private use.

Since all were now staying for weekends the fees were raised to £2 yearly though it was acknowledged that not all fees would be forthcoming. Fees in other boarding schools for African children ranged from £2 to £6, while the average annual income of the African was £12.

In July 1937 Doctor and his family returned from his first furlough. While in Scotland, he had given most interesting and informative talks about the Mission and put the need for a new well before the people. He told them: "The whole work of the Mission revolves round this question of water." The people, as usual, most generously provided the necessary funds. He and Mr Tallach set about the work, and soon the well was ready for use, yielding up to 1000 gallons a day. The pump was worked by an engine, and a large storage tank further eased problems. So there were now two wells! All rejoiced as only those can who have experienced a severe shortage of water.

Doctor was living with a growing family in a house that was far too small – just two corrugated iron huts, very rickety and half-eaten by white ants. A new house was overdue and work began. "I have laid strong concrete over the foundations and have gone to the expense of laying a metal ant-course under the brick-work," he wrote. "All the windows too are of steel and, although cost is high, we do not anticipate further trouble, while wood casements are soon

A HEART FOR AFRICA

destroyed by ants and weather. The bricks are of course "green" or unburnt, and the roof will be grass thatch. I have tried to keep down expenses, buying old doors and patching them up." He had an eye for design and the resultant sturdy, pleasing house with handsome Dutch gable lent an air of mild grandeur to the Mission compound and stood for over 60 years. In the event, thatch was unobtainable so it had a corrugated iron roof, not so picturesque but what it lost in beauty it gained in permanence.

It was a happy day when the family moved in, but especially so perhaps for Mrs Macdonald. Practical and energetic, kindly and ready-to-be-happy, she was an excellent house-keeper with high standards – characteristics which must have both helped and irked when she had to cope in the dilapidated little huts.

At Ingwenya the buildings eventually formed a circle round a large open space. To prevent erosion, large Australian gum trees were planted. They grew up very tall, giants among the smaller native trees and shrubs: the mopani – beautifully shaped with a horizontal spread – and the flamboyant and the flaming red hibiscus.

The house with the Dutch gable, built by Dr MacDonald in the late 1930s.
It lasted until the end of the century when it was replaced by a new house.
Standing in the foreground are Katie Macaulay, Jean and Sheila Macleod.

To interest the parents, a show of work was held at the end of term, when prizes were presented by Patrick Mzamo, the senior elder. Crochet, bead-work, jerseys, socks and scarves were admired. There were four wool rugs, wooden stools, three-legged clay pots and large baskets made of ilala – a palm-leaf from far-off Shangani. The prizes were such commodities as nail brushes, toothbrushes, towels, cakes of soap – all highly valued. Tea was served and the parents went home well-pleased.

The years so full of interest, and occasional loneliness, sped by and by early 1938 Jean and her mother were looking forward to their leave. They had been momentous years in the history of the school. It had developed into a well-run establishment of which the Inspectors spoke most appreciatively. With her willing helpers and staff, the headmistress had set a standard which was to characterise it to a greater or lesser extent into the next century.

The harmony and co-operation between the missionaries owed much to their character and to the sensible working practices they adopted. Mr Tallach, older than the others, had a wide experience of life, having rubbed shoulders with all sorts of people. Also each had his own distinct sphere of expertise and, importantly, the others recognised it. Where skill was lacking they improvised as best they could, believing that rough-and-ready solutions to problems were better than none. Where work overlapped there was tolerance. Being at one and the same time idealists and realists, they pulled together in a common purpose – that African girls might be brought to Christ. "And no higher aim," said Mr Tallach, "can be asked of us, and a better reason for having a boarding school cannot be found."

Jean's annual reports reflect some of the lively interest and freshness of view of the newcomer and the eye she had for putting her readers in the picture. She wrote, "It is difficult to give an adequate idea of the vast field of opportunity there is . . . in all branches of educational work, of how little is being accomplished, and of the absorbing interest which makes the work its own reward."

While Jean went on leave, her place was to be taken by James Fraser, a native of Strathpeffer. After graduating with an Arts degree from Glasgow University, he trained as a teacher and had taught for two years in Scotland. On being asked to go to Ingwenya he readily agreed.

Before going home Jean informed the Committee that she was willing to return for a further spell of duty. On 3rd June she and her mother set sail for Scotland. The Committee decided as a gesture of appreciation to pay Mrs Nicolson's fare both ways – but she refused it, insisting that the money be paid instead to the Mission. So it was sent out for Doctor to use, as he had plans for converting his old house into a small hospital with an operating room and a maternity unit.

CHAPTER 8

First Leave and Return to Ingwenya

JEAN and her mother arrived in Scotland with the clouds of war looming ominously on the horizon. An absence of five years had brought many changes. George V had died in 1936, the abdication of Edward VIII was a thing of the past and George VI and his queen Elizabeth with the little princesses projected an ideal of wholesome family life.

They were glad to be reunited with family and friends and especially to have Mackinlay with them again. For some weeks they rented a house in Lochinver. Mrs Nicolson's brother Murdo and his wife lived in the family home in Inverkirkaig and Jean enjoyed meeting up with cousins.

They then moved to Glasgow. In St Jude's there was a new minister. After Rev Neil Cameron's death in 1932, Rev Roderick Mackenzie had been called to the large congregation. He was a gifted preacher whose ministry they greatly appreciated. As he had visited the Mission in 1929 he was naturally eager to hear of the latest developments. Everywhere they went, they were asked about the Mission and, in an informal way, they generated much interest. They had brought with them a model of a kraal and other artefacts, with examples of work done by the schoolchildren.

Rumours of war persisted despite Chamberlain's promise of "peace in our time" guaranteed by the Munich Agreement of

September 1938, when the British Prime Minister accepted Hitler's annexation of southern Czechoslovakia. Even those who lacked direct experience of the carnage of the Great War were eager to believe the good news. When, the following March, Hitler broke the Munich Pact by a further invasion of Czechoslovakia the outbreak of war seemed imminent. Air-raid shelters were built, gas masks distributed and classes in first aid organised. The thoughts of mother and sister were much with Mackinlay, who had recently gone to the United States, from where he was pursuing his career at sea. Jean had a great concern for his spiritual welfare and used to send him notes of sermons of Rev N Cameron and Rev R Mackenzie.

Mrs Nicolson decided she could not think of returning to Africa without seeing him again, so in August she set off across the Atlantic. On arriving in New York, she found billboards shouting the news that Hitler had invaded Poland. Britain and France declared war on Germany on 3 September 1939. She tried to make arrangements to return immediately but was informed that no passage would be available for at least a year.

Jean was due to return to Africa in December but, in view of the danger from mines and from the German U-boats which were attacking an ill-prepared Navy and merchant shipping in the Atlantic, the Committee advised her not to sail meantime. They undertook to continue her salary till such time as she should find a post at home.

Jean gladly accepted the kind offer of the MacAskill sisters in Glasgow to have her stay with them – the only snag being that the windows of her apartment were not blacked out as was required in view of expected air attacks. So Jean set off down Byres Road in search of the material with which to make the mandatory blinds. Marching back with the tell-tale roll under her arm, she met a typically friendly Glaswegian who shook his head understandingly: "He's an awfu' man Hitler!"

Britain was arming with all speed. Shipbuilders in Clydebank and Port Glasgow were working flat out; aircraft carriers, destroyers and vital merchant ships were being hastily fitted out and smaller craft converted to military use. The terrible toll on shipping was eased somewhat by the expedient of sailing in convoy. And the Committee, in view of the fact that this arrangement seemed to offer a degree of

The Clyde in more peaceful times – in 1939, "shipbuilders . . . were working flat out".

safety, advised Jean early in 1940 that, if she wished to return to Africa, they would agree – but she must feel under no compulsion whatsoever; the decision was entirely hers.

After much heart-searching and prayer she decided to go. It was a brave decision, for she was nervous, as anyone living near the busy Clyde might well be. Years later she was to recall, "I was afraid – not so much that the ship might be attacked, though I was afraid of that. No, it was less the fear of dying itself that concerned me than the question of whether I was ready to face death – what lay after death." At this time her minister visited the house where she was staying and she was impressed and encouraged by words from Micah which he quoted in prayer; "Who is a God like unto thee, that pardoneth iniquity, and passeth by the transgression of the remnant of his heritage? He retaineth not his anger for ever, because He delighteth in mercy."

"I will never forget it," said Jean. "He read a chapter from Deuteronomy - all the blessings. My aunt travelled down to London with me and we stayed with Dr Tallach. He read that same chapter. Next morning I said goodbye, went down to Southampton, got

A HEART FOR AFRICA

aboard ship and I hadn't a fear. I was sure it was because of the prayers of the people at home. I was as happy as I was at any time – all fear gone. The Captain called us together and told us that we were not going to wait for a convoy but would zig-zag out into the Atlantic."

It was in late March she sailed and she arrived safely at Ingwenya in mid-April. Mr Tallach reported, "We all thought Miss Nicolson very brave in her return to us through the ocean battle-area. She got a real Ingwenya welcome. Over three hundred children, strung out along the road from the mission gate, waited to cheer her back to work."

Much had changed. Of immediate relevance were the renovations to her "wee jewel of a house", as young Catherine Tallach, who was to stay with Jean meantime, remembered it. Dr Macdonald and Mr Tallach had done all they could to make it comfortable and attractive. It had been rethatched and it now had the luxury of a ceiling! And the trees! Over a hundred had been planted. And there was a flourishing school garden with potatoes, cabbages, onions, spinach, peas, beans and much else. James Fraser had evidently thrown himself into the work with enthusiasm and he obligingly remained in the school for ten days as he handed over to Jean.

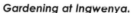

Gardening at Ingwenya.

At the outbreak of war James had tried to make arrangements for returning to Scotland in order to enlist in the armed forces but was refused permission by the Government. As he had shown himself a gifted and energetic teacher and had gained the respect of the education authorities, he was asked to take up an appointment as Master of Methods at Hope Fountain Mission, ten miles south of Bulawayo, where his expertise was put to good use in the training of African teachers. So successful was he that his methods were eventually adopted throughout Southern Rhodesia. Whenever feasible he visited Ingwenya, proving to be a welcome and refreshing guest, and helped out by keeping church services both there and at out-lying stations. It was while at Hope Fountain that he was given the name which stuck and was so appropriate, Thandabantu, the man who loves the people.

If the pupils were sorry to say goodbye to their headmaster, they were delighted to have Misi back among them and eager to tell her how they had come out top in arithmetic in Matabeleland. Not only that, but they had distinguished themselves in a writing competition on the subject of veldt fires; five out of eleven prizes had come to Ingwenya!

"While we were at home," Jean wrote, "Mrs Tallach and Mrs Macdonald took full responsibility for the needlework, laundry and cookery classes. They spared no pains in teaching and helping the local teachers, and Miss Rudd, our Government Inspectress, highly commended all the work done." Being enthusiastic teachers they had the happy knack of enthusing their pupils. The girls made their own clothes and enjoyed adding individual touches of cross-stitch or embroidery. Soon they had acquired a Singer sewing machine for the use of the upper classes – and a few years later, to the joy of the girls, another.

To Jean the charge of the school seemed a much more daunting undertaking than when she had first arrived. There were now over 400 pupils with eight teachers. As before she had a full-time teaching commitment in addition to the overall responsibility.

James Fraser had described the numbers in school as "well-nigh unwieldy", and year by year they continued to rise. The classrooms could not contain them and soon they were spilling over into one of the dormitories. And what time was wasted juggling furniture, matching desks to chairs to boys!

"Misi, my chair is too low!"

"Misi, I can't get my legs under the desk!"

Off went Mfundisi. He managed to track down 20 combined desks and seats in a European school in town that was refurbishing – all for a bargain £20, which had been gifted. Oh the ongoing joy of those desks! Another time he came home in triumph with cupboards and desks from an air base near Bulawayo.

Though more boys were coming to school than formerly, girls still predominated. The irregular attendance of the boys who did come continued to be one of the biggest problems. They came as day-pupils but were 12 before they came to school and were very shy, according to Jean. The younger boys were required at home to herd the sheep and goats, ensuring that they did not wander into the cultivated fields. The older lads had the privilege of caring for the cattle – and privilege it was because cattle were the wealth of the Matabele and were the province of the men; women were not even allowed into the cattle kraal. The oxen had their own names and were the men's special pride. Every Friday the boys took the animals to be dipped, and twice a week during the dry season they drove them to a river five miles off to be watered. Naturally their progress in school suffered.

Jean described a Beginners' class of small children – local children were all small until they reached the age of 13 or 14 – "The boys in this class have spent four or five years as herd-boys before coming to school. Armed with long sticks they have driven the cattle out on the veldt each morning, and returned with them in the evening. They have spent the day clambering on the backs of the oxen, setting the bulls of rival herds to fight, racing on the calves and donkeys, and stealing honey from the wild bees' hives. Is it any wonder that, when they come to school, they find it much easier to scramble over one another's backs than to walk in normal fashion across the floor? The little girls have had, on the whole, a less turbulent childhood. For the last few years they have helped the mother to look after the younger children and have had almost invariably a baby strapped on their backs."

One memorable day a gift of money arrived from the North Uist congregation for the boys! The boys had never before received a gift earmarked for them and were enormously pleased. Spades and hoes were bought and Paul Hlazo soon had them planting corn and beans. And there was cash to spare for tools for simple woodwork, a change from bits of glass and home-made adzes which till then had sufficed for shaping stools, wooden spoons and clubs.

On her rounds one morning Jean dropped in on Abia Sobantu's class. Like Zacchaeus he was very short of stature and that morning she found herself getting very short with him as she watched from the side of the room while he proceeded with his lesson. The more he explained, the more confused the pupils became. Jean could stand it no longer. "Mr Sobantu, I shall take the class now, if you please," and she stepped forward to undo the damage. After some disentangling of muddledom she said, "Now we'll work out an

1949 group. Patrick Mzamo, aged 86, is seated; to his right and left are Jean and Jessie Nicolson; his son, Petros, who taught with Mr Fraser, stands in the doorway; standing in front of him is Abia Sobantu; on the right are Mr Mzamo's two daughters-in-law.

A HEART FOR AFRICA

example on the blackboard!" But she couldn't get at the blackboard for the clutter of boxes in front of it – an affront to her sense of decorum! "And what are these boxes doing here? You two boys, will you take them away, please, right outside!" The lesson continued and then she said, "Now, Mr Sobantu, you will perhaps do the next example with them on the blackboard," handing the chalk to him. A hapless Mr Sobantu wailed, "But you kicked my boxes out and I can't reach the blackboard!"

Jean used to enjoy telling the story against herself and declaring what a fine Christian and teacher he was as well as an eager, lively and warm-hearted friend; "one of nature's gentlemen," she commented. Like many attending the church, he was a Fingo from the nearby Maqaqeni Reserve and had been converted through Mr Tallach's ministry. Some years previously as he listened to Mr Tallach the words, "Against thee, thee only, have I sinned, and done this evil in thy sight," had convinced him that he was indeed a sinner and needed a Saviour. Another sermon, on the verse, "The peace of God, which passeth all understanding, shall keep your hearts and minds through Christ Jesus," brought that peace to his heart. Since he had a beautiful voice and was a trained singer, he conducted a singing class on Friday evenings and led the singing in church. The congregation sang heartily and most melodiously, the rich tones rising and falling with improvised part-singing.

Attendance at church was an integral part of the school year. The Sabbath day began with a prayer meeting at 8 o'clock attended by boarders and day pupils, as well as people from the surrounding kraals. Sabbath school followed, superintended by Doctor. After the formal opening, the various groups dispersed to their classrooms, where the teaching was based on the Bible; in addition, the *Westminster Shorter Catechism* was discussed with the seniors. At around 11 o'clock the bell clanged out – an iron rod striking an empty oil drum – to let it be known that the first church service of the day would begin soon, at 11.30. There was a second service at 2pm, so the people generally sat around between the services, and after the afternoon service they made for home before darkness fell. In term time a third service was held in early evening for the boarders and teachers. It was in English. The order of service was in each case as in the church in Scotland. The whole school and a number of adults attended the Thursday morning prayer meeting.

Mfundisi or Doctor usually preached, but if they were away on trek, Mr Fraser or an elder would take the services. One of the elders, Patrick Mzamo, a tall spare man with a commanding presence, had been one of Mr Radasi's helpers. Although quite frail, he said of himself, "When I preach, I feel like a racehorse, I must go all out or not go at all." Women, many of them mothers with babies sleeping contentedly on their backs, sat on one side of the church, men on the other, while younger children squatted on the floor at the front. There was little disturbance, though the iron-clad church in the centre of the compound could scarcely hold all who came; perhaps a mother would quietly go out with a fractious child or a dog might wander in.

In school there was the daily Scripture lesson, which James Fraser described as "a little sermon in itself, for most of our teachers are Church members and they do not hesitate to apply gospel truths to the hearts and consciences of the children". He added, "Mr Tallach holds a special meeting with the boarders every Friday evening. He gives them a heart-to-heart talk on sin and salvation, and that Friday meeting has been blessed to the conversion of not a few wayward girls."

The Lord's Supper was celebrated in the congregation twice a year, in March and September. A typical Communion season was described by Amelia Mthamo, a girl in Standard 6 who had become a member in the church the previous autumn. "Write a letter to friends in Scotland telling them about our Communion services," the class was told. Amelia's was chosen as the best and incidentally it gives some indication of the standard of English attained by a good pupil.

"I would like to tell you about our communion season here at Ingwenya. We began our services on Thursday, which is our baptizing day. On that day many babies and three schoolgirls were baptised. Doctor Macdonald preached. He explained what baptism is, and as I was listening, I heard him say that baptism was a sign of being baptised with the Holy Ghost, and is given to those who prefer to follow the Lord Jesus Christ than to walk in the ways of the world. He read from the Book of Psalms, Psalm 51, verse 7, which says: 'Purge me with hyssop and I shall be clean; wash me, and I shall be

Ladies at an Ingwenya communion.

whiter than snow.' On Friday we held a prayer meeting at which Mr Tallach read three psalms from the book of Psalms, and six men prayed. They all prayed that the Holy Ghost would be poured on themselves and on the people. On Saturday we had the usual preparation service. Many people assembled for the first service on Sabbath, when Mr Tallach preached on Matthew chapter 27, verse 36. Before the second service the followers of Jesus were given tokens and, after Doctor Macdonald had preached in Isaiah chapter 55, verse 1, we took the Lord's Supper. We were happy when we remembered all that Jesus has done for us. On Monday we had a thanksgiving service to thank God for his kindness during the communion. I was thanking God for giving us peace when so many people in other lands are being killed in war. I was also very glad because thirteen schoolgirls became members at this communion season. I hope you may have a happy time, my friends, when you remember the death of the Lord Jesus."

In James' opinion the boarding-school system had been "very successful so far as the formation of strong Christian character is concerned". He noted that when young people "come and stay in a place where they get systematic instruction in the Word of God and where, in spite of frailties and weaknesses, they see something of the glory of Christ in the daily life of teachers, missionaries, elders and church members, that makes an impression and lays a foundation which no amount of mere preaching can ever do. That is the justification for our having a boarding school at Ingwenya, and we have been amply rewarded as a church by the fact that not a few of these girls have gone forth to heathen districts as 'missionaries'. They have carried the gospel to their homes and communities, often in the face of much and bitter opposition. Mr Tallach remarked to me more than once last year how encouraged he was to find that young men and women who had been brought up in the school, and had left and had fallen into loose ways of living, were coming back and showing a thirst for what they had been taught in their early days."

Mr Tallach told of a Christian girl who was ill, "a quiet respectful lassie much loved by all. As it became clear to her parents, who are good people, that she was to leave them, they naturally began to weep. On seeing this she called her mother and told her to turn up the fourteenth chapter of John and to read it aloud. After this was done, Simangaliso asked her mother whose words were these and at what time did Jesus say them. When she received correct answers she said, 'I did not ask you to read that chapter for my sake but for yours. I know that I am going to Jesus and, just as He left these comforting words with His disciples, so now I leave them with you. Since He left such comforting words as these, it is not proper of you to be too much grieved because I am leaving you. Do not cry too much for me. I am happy and I am going to be much happier still.' Shortly after this she died."

He remarked that in past years a congregation would consist mainly of true believers, their children and interested heathen, whereas now it also included those who had been baptized and had renounced heathenish ways but were not true Christians. The presence of nominal Christians in the church was thus a comparatively new phenomenon.

As the weeks passed without news of her mother, Jean became increasingly anxious. Months passed and still no word. A special prayer-meeting for the war was held regularly at Ingwenya and naturally Mrs Nicolson was much in the thoughts of all. Then one glad day in mid-October, word came that she was on her way to Bembesi, was arriving that very afternoon! They went to meet her and found her hale and hearty and grateful to be back on African soil. The Mission family, European and African alike, received her with much jubilation and thanksgiving. The welcome from Patrick Mzamo, aged 86, expressed the feelings of all. Jean remembered how he was one of the first to call to see her mother; "she was resting that afternoon, and I took him into the bedroom. He ignored mother's outstretched hand but dropped to his knees in the doorway and gave thanks to the Lord for her safe keeping. Then he rose and shook her warmly by the hand."

And what a tale she had to tell! With her sharp memory and eye for detail, she made it live for her listeners. Though far removed from the scene of war, they got a first-hand insight into the conflict and felt some of the atmosphere of hostilities. She had seen her brothers in Canada and had met up with Mackinlay. She had visited friends in Toronto, with the result that a support group was formed which, year by year, faithfully sent much-appreciated goods and money to the Mission. All this was relayed graphically, and as eagerly digested. And then her adventures at sea had begun.

Standing, left to right: Deacons – Timothy Moyo, Daniel Moyo, Simangalesi, Madema, Simon Mpofu, Simon Moyo. Seated: Elders – John Mthambo, Patrick Mzamo, John Sabwenga, Amos Ngombane.

● CHAPTER 9 ●

Mother's Adventures at Sea

WHAT follows is an account of Mrs Nicolson's experiences at sea as she returned from the United States to Africa in 1940. Like the narrative of her parents' life in Arizona, the story is as Jean told it to her friends.

●

In July 1939 Mother and I had been at home in Scotland, chiefly in Glasgow, for over a year. Six months before my brother, Mackinlay, had been with us, undecided as to what to do. He had been serving in the British merchant service since the age of 17 and was a Second Officer, but he was now told that he would not be allowed to sit his First Officer's certificate since he had been born in America. So he had gone off to the Gulf of Mexico, to Mobile, Alabama, where we had a cousin, Captain Norman Nicolson, director of a shipping company.

It would soon be time for me to return to Southern Rhodesia and Mother was coming too. However, she had a great longing to see my brother and decided to pay a brief visit to Canada and America. She wished me to accompany her but Aunt Johan was so distressed at the thought of our returning to Africa that I decided not to go, even though Mackinlay offered to pay my fare. However, his ship unexpectedly called in at London and he paid a hurried visit to Glasgow. We were grateful to have these few days together. "My ship often calls in at Cape Town and," he promised; "the first time I manage to get leave, I'll go up to Ingwenya."

As soon as war was declared, I received a cable from Mother which read, "Returning immediately". However, she discovered that it was impossible to secure a passage, as all berths were required for British men returning to the UK. Since there was no possibility of securing a berth for at least a year, she spent some time with Mackinlay as a guest on his ship, on which he was First Officer. She then went on to visit her brothers, all four of them settled in Canada. She stayed in Sudbury with Donald and family and then proceeded to Saskatchewan to see Dan and George, and their families. Then it was off to Vancouver, where Bill then lived. Next stop was Seattle, where she still had a few friends. From Seattle she travelled to San Francisco, where most of my father's relatives lived. She told me that, if I had been with her, we should have gone on to Tucson.

In July 1940 Mother returned to New York and set about securing a passage to South Africa. She was told that there was a berth available on a small Dutch trader, the *SS Kertosone*, which was soon to leave New Orleans for Durban. It carried 12 passengers. Mother made her way to New Orleans, where she found placards on the streets announcing that France had fallen to the Nazis and Italy had entered the War.

She shared a cabin with a young missionary, Miss Schmalenberger, of German origin but now settled in the United States. Because there were so few passengers, they and the officers had meals at the Captain's table. Mother commented later that the Captain and men were courtesy itself.

One day Mother was sitting in the saloon when she noticed a man painting the windows with grey paint.

"Are you expecting trouble?" she enquired. "

No, Madam," he replied, "but it is best to be prepared."

By this time Germany had overrun Holland without warning. The United States had not yet entered the fray. Two of the passengers were Jewish men who had escaped from Europe but had been refused asylum in America and hoped to find refuge in South Africa. There were two young students from South Africa with British passports. A missionary couple with a ten-month-old baby were on their way to a mission station in the Belgian Congo, and Miss Schmalenberger was travelling with them.

A week out to sea, they were at the Captain's table having lunch when there was a tremendous roar. The vessel trembled. In a moment Captain and officers had disappeared. The passengers looked at one another and followed the men. When they reached the deck, they saw what Mother said was the ugliest sight she had ever seen. It was a large vessel with black sails riding high on the sea, about 300 yards away.

"What is that?" she asked one of the men.

"A German raider, Madam," he replied. "They have shot across our bows and they are going to sink the ship. They have also sent a message not to destroy any papers – but the Captain has destroyed everything by now. You had better go to your cabin and take a small case and any small thing you value. Put on a warm coat. We are going to get into the lifeboats."

Mother went down to the cabin. Her companion, Miss Schmalenberger, was sitting motionless. Mother took a small case and put her Bible in it. She forgot that she was going to be in mid-Atlantic and put her nightdress and toilet-bag in next. She then noticed a thin coat she'd bought in New York and slipped into it – and put a warm coat on top of it. She then stuffed a piece of material, also bought in New York, up her sleeve. Mother was now conscious of the German girl watching her.

"Aren't you going to try to save something?" Mother enquired.

"No, we are told to take the spoiling of our goods cheerfully and I am not going to try to save anything. Besides," she added, "how are you going to get into the lifeboat wearing all these clothes?" Then she added, "The ship belongs to the Germans now."

"It does not belong to the Germans!" Mother replied. "It is a Dutch ship."

Mother felt a bit ashamed of herself and took the material out from her sleeve. She went up on deck again. The raider was now much closer. A rope ladder was slung over the side of the ship and some seamen were climbing up, carrying something.

"What are they carrying?" Mother enquired of an officer who was standing beside her.

"These are German officers, Madam," he replied, "and they are carrying time-bombs to sink the ship."

Mother joined a group of passengers standing at one side of the deck. She was startled to see the Jews weeping. Mr Yoder was holding his little boy of ten months also weeping; but his wife was quite calm. The two British students from South Africa were not to be seen – they were already in custody. Mother now began to comfort the poor Jews, who had gone through so much already. She said afterwards that Bible verses came rushing into her mind.

"We do not need to be afraid of them," she said. "They cannot do anything to us except what the Lord will allow them. You know what it says in the Word of God, 'The nations of the earth are but the small dust of the balance, and but a drop in the bucket.' 'And now even at this present time, mine head shall lifted be above all those that are my foes and round encompass me,'" quoting Psalm 27. Suddenly she was aware that they were all staring at her and she withdrew into the background.

One of the Dutch officers told her, "The Germans have found that we have a valuable cargo of oil on board. They are very short of oil so they are not going to sink the ship after all. They are going to take us to Lorient in western France. So, Mrs Nicolson, you can go back to your cabin and take off your coat. The German Commander is on board and he has taken the passports." When Mother returned to the deck the German Commander was examining the passports.

"Where is the British lady?" he enquired. Mother stepped forward and Mrs Yoder, the missionary's wife, stepped forward also and stood beside her.

"Mrs Nicolson is travelling with us," she said. "We are all going to the mission field."

"You are British?" the Commander said to Mother.

"Yes," Mother replied.

"Why does it say on your passport, 'widow of an American citizen,' if you are British?"

"My husband was also British but he emigrated to the United States and, in order to get command of a ship, he had to become an American citizen."

"I see. Then why do you say you are British?"

"Because I was born in Scotland."

"We do not care where you were born," the Commander replied. "Are you British or are you American? If you are British, we cannot let you go."

"Are you going to throw me overboard?" enquired Mother.

"No, but you are going to have a taste of war."

"Well," said Mother, "It is wartime!" When I heard of Mother's impertinence I was shocked!

Next morning Mother was summoned by the German Commander.

"Mrs Nicolson, you give us much trouble. We do not know whether you are British or American. We have cabled to Paris about you." The Germans were anxious to keep America out of the war – and they didn't want to risk imprisoning Mother if she was American.

That morning Mother met the Dutch captain on deck, looking worried.

"Mrs Nicolson, if I did not have a wife and children in Rotterdam I would kill that man for stealing my ship."

"Oh well, Captain, I'm in the soup," Mother said.

"In the soup, Mrs Nicolson?"

"Yes, they have cabled to Paris about me. Anyone in the consular service there will know very well that I am British. My passport is navy blue. The Americans have red passports."

"Never mind, Mrs Nicolson, you have told them the truth; they cannot do anything to you. The German officers are speaking quite freely to my officers. They are telling my men where they have been and the ships they have sunk. I am going to pass on the information to you and you will report it to the first British Consul you meet."

"Oh," said mother, "I'll write it down."

"Oh no, you will write nothing! You must memorise it. Every day I'll tell you a little." So each morning they met on deck and the Captain told Mother a little more. The raider was disguised as a banana boat. It had two planes below the hatches. They had sunk two British ships in the River Plate, and so on.

When they arrived in Lorient they heard they were going on to Paris. A German chauffeur was to drive them in the large car that the American missionaries had on board for use on the Mission Field.

They spent several days on the way. Every time they arrived at a hotel, the German chauffeur bowed and said, "You are now the guests of the German Army." But the guests had to pay the bill themselves!

They passed through villages destroyed by bombs and every time the officer would point out the devastation and say, "German bombs! German bombs!" They stopped at several army camps. At one camp, a young German apprentice goose-stepped up to Mother and said, "You are English."

"No, I am Scottish."

"It is all the same! England is finished. Two weeks more and England is finished, and then the Duke of Windsor will be king. He is a friend of Germany."

Mother did not know whether or not he was telling the truth.

Eventually they arrived in Paris. By now Mother was feeling very despondent. She wondered if she would be put in a concentration camp.

There was no room for her in the same hotel as the Americans, but next morning they called for her. They were by this time calling her "Auntie".

"Come along, Auntie, we're all going to the American consul to have our photographs taken for our new passports."

"There is no use my going to the American Consul," Mother said. "He will know at once that I am British."

"You come with us," they said.

The German chauffeur followed them everywhere, but on this occasion, when they entered the Consul's office, he was deep in conversation with another German and was paying no attention to them. The Consul looked at the passports.

"Who is the lady with the British passport?" he asked. Mother stepped forward. One of the ladies said, "Mrs Nicolson is passing as an American citizen."

"Oh, I see! How did you get this far with a British passport?" he asked.

"By the prayers of the people in Scotland," she replied.

"If that is the case . . . " and he stamped the passport AMERICAN. She was now under the protection of the United States of America. However, the Consul remarked to one of the missionaries that he was sorry for the British lady. They would have to pass through several army camps, one of them Spanish. "She'll never get through the Spanish camp," he said. "They are very keen to please the Germans."

The next day they set off for Lisbon, Portugal. At various military camps they had to hand in their passports, but at the Spanish border they were ordered into the office. When it came to Mother's turn, the man behind the counter said, "I am sorry, Madam, you will have to pay ten dollars." Mother couldn't get the money out quickly enough! They were on their way to Lisbon, free to go to where they would! However, Lisbon was overflowing with refugees and Mother was told she would have to remain in Coimbra, a small town near Lisbon, for five weeks. The Americans were allowed to proceed.

Mother's money was running out by now. She bought a small methylated-spirit stove, a bottle of spirit, a small pan and a packet of tea. Every morning she bought rolls, tomatoes and milk. That is what she had every morning – every meal actually – a roll, a tomato and a cup of tea. Eventually the five weeks were over and she was permitted to leave for Lisbon.

While in Lisbon, one of the American missionaries said to Mother, "We are going to visit two ladies who run a school for English children. Would you like to come with us?" There they met a Portuguese gentleman who had just been visiting the prison to see Alves Reis, whose story he then told. He had been a swindler who had persuaded hundreds of people to invest in a bogus company. When his crime was detected he was imprisoned for 25 years.

While he was in prison, someone handed in tracts. Being at a loose end he read them and then asked for a Bible; he had never seen one. The upshot was that he was converted and his whole life changed. He began to take an interest in his fellow-prisoners and a number of them were converted. When, some years later, he was offered his freedom he refused it. He said he would never again have as good an opportunity to help the prisoners. Mother was most interested, as she had read the story in the *Evangelical Quarterly*.

Mother kept enquiring at Thomas Cook's about a passage to South Africa. One morning she received a phone call to say that a small Portuguese vessel would be sailing in a day or two. If a passage was available they would definitely phone her by 10 o'clock that evening. So Mother sat in the vestibule of the hotel awaiting the call. 10 o'clock came; no call. 10.30; still no call. 11 o'clock; 11.30. She went up to her room. She had forgotten there was a telephone in her room. Soon it rang.

"Is that Mrs Nicolson?"

"Yes."

"I'm sorry to be so late but . . . "

"Oh, that doesn't matter in the least."

"Madam, will you let me speak, please? You may have a passage on the ship leaving tomorrow night but you must not go on board until after midnight."

"Oh, thank you very much!"

She duly got on board and was escorted to her cabin. Two ladies were asleep in their bunks at one side of the cabin. Mother was shown a little couch with a pillow, and a rug thrown over it. It was very warm that evening and the door was hooked back with a curtain hung across the doorway.

The ship set sail. It dipped this way and dipped that way and rolled from side to side. The couch was upholstered with a smooth polished leather and every time the ship lurched to one side Mother slid off! At length she sat up and looked at her watch. It was 2am.

She was facing the door and all of a sudden she noticed a man's hand come round the curtain. She then saw a pair of feet protruding under it. "Someone coming to rob the cabin!" thought Mother. "I'll be there before him!" She leapt up and whisked back the curtain. There stood a smallish Jewish man with a bald head, in his pyjamas, his mouth open in astonishment.

"What do you want?" Mother demanded.

"I want to see my wife," he replied.

"At 2 o'clock in the morning?" said my mother.

"I want to see my wife. . . ." he repeated.

"Certainly not!"

"I've a . . . "

"Get away," my mother said, "or I'll have you put away." The man went away. Mother was now wide awake, her nerves on edge.

Next morning she went up on deck and joined a group of ladies seated together. She was not long seated when she saw the unmistakeable figure of the Jewish man of the night before. He came over to her.

"You are the lady who would not allow me to enter my wife's cabin."

"Yes, I am. Whoever heard of a gentleman coming to a lady's cabin at two in the morning?"

"I wanted to give my wife medicine," he said.

"Why did you not say so?"

"You would not let me speak!"

"Why did you not knock on the door?" asked one of the ladies.

"I knock on the curtain," he said. Everybody laughed. So I said to Mother long afterwards, "I hope you apologised."

"No, I didn't," she said.

"Oh well," I said, "that was dreadful."

After he had gone, the ladies told Mother that he and his wife had escaped across the Pyrenees when France was invaded. His wife was expecting a baby and was supposed to have medication every two or three hours.

The *Gao Bello* had now reached Cape Town, and Mother was longing to set foot on British soil, but the ship continued on her way. It went round the coast and eventually reached Beira, Portuguese East Africa. From there Mother cabled to Bembesi, saying that she was arriving that afternoon. Rev John Tallach, Dr MacDonald and I met the train and Mother arrived looking pale but cool and collected.

● CHAPTER 10 ●

Sorrows of War

AT Ingwenya there was always work to be done and soon Mrs Nicolson was immersed in teaching to such effect that she was appointed a Domestic Science teacher, unpaid, by the Foreign Missions Committee subject to the Department's approval.

Jean had brought from home a new luxury, a wireless set. It was a little thing and "crackled like mad" according to Catherine Tallach but it was a link with the outside world. It was the first radio to appear at the Mission and was hugely appreciated especially by Doctor and Mr Tallach, who had always taken a keen interest in world affairs and had their opinions about everything. Every evening 9 o'clock saw them make their way to the Nicolson home to listen, ears straining, to the news. Sometimes Paul Hlazo came too and many were the animated discussions as they followed the progress of the war on the wall map that Mrs Nicolson had brought with her. These listening-in sessions were something of a highlight in their busy lives and it meant that throughout the war they had a fair idea of what was going on. The Mission personnel all had relatives and friends who were facing danger at the Front or in their homes.

The Nicolsons were very much aware of the peril Mackinlay faced on the high seas and anxiously awaited each letter. Mail was disrupted so that letters went missing or were months in arriving. Little wonder the Mission folk experienced a sense of isolation. One letter from Winnipeg arrived blotted and travel-stained and bearing the stamp, Salved from the Sea, a poignant reminder of the hazards of the way.

The local population, too, was affected by the war. Many of the pupils had fathers and brothers helping in the war effort. There was a large Royal Air Force training centre near Bulawayo. The boarders were busy knitting socks and other woollies for the troops. There were shortages. It was difficult to get material for the sewing classes so during the war years the parcels that came from Canada were doubly precious. Petrol was rationed. Food was rationed and expensive and Mrs Radasi, the boarding mistress, had to tell the girls, "From next week we will have two meals a day instead of three."

This is where the school garden came into its own. Gardening had been made a compulsory subject for girls. Erosion was a serious problem in the Reserve. Indiscriminate cutting down of trees for fuel and, to a lesser extent, building had denuded the ground. The system of agriculture was also wasteful so, since that was women's work, it was logical to educate the girls in a better way of managing the land.

Simon Moyo, a former pupil trained in agriculture, now a teacher and a member in the Ingwenya congregation, was in charge. He first set the little boys to plant a rubber-plant hedge by the fence which surrounded the Mission. A quick-growing shrub, it should eventually strengthen the fence and keep goats and other animals out. The boys worked with a will and at Simon's suggestion they were rewarded by a feast of stewed goat and bread! It was proposed to follow a four-crop rotation system. Simon worked long after his official hours, often staying on the Mission until dusk ensuring that the vegetable plots and fruit trees were watered in the cool of the day. There were over 40 small fruit trees – peaches, guavas, paw-paws. Over a thousand tomatoes were raised on the girls' plots as well as peas, beans and other crops.

Water was a problem. In calm weather the windmill came to a standstill and there was no water to spare for the garden. The girls then had to carry water from another well at least a quarter of a mile off. That took most of the afternoon. They experimented with different crops and came to the conclusion that citrus fruits required too much water, so they settled for a purely guava orchard. Animals

A HEART FOR AFRICA

School garden with protective hedge.

were another problem. Sometimes the garden gate was left open and the cattle made the most of their opportunity. All in all, however, the venture was a success.

Setting out on a stroll one afternoon, Jean and her mother met some of the boarder girls effortlessly carrying pumpkins on their heads. Jean hurried in for her camera and got a snap of a delighted group. Some of these pumpkins weighed anything up to 30 pounds. They were the girls' own produce and made a healthful addition to the dinner menu. One year they grew 50!

Doctor was delighted with these developments and observed that since vegetable-growing had taken off, pellagra and scurvy had become a thing of the past. Unusually there was, however, an outbreak of malaria soon after Jean's arrival and many of the boarder girls were affected. Jean wrote, "Last year we lost a very nice girl in Standard 6 through malaria. She had been at Ingwenya as a boarder for over two years but was a member in the Church of England. She was only a few days ill. Her last words were, 'This world is not good. Heaven is good.'"

The summers of 1942 and 1943 were dry and Matabeleland experienced severe drought. No rain fell for months on end and the ground was black and scorched. Over 600 cattle died in the small reserve and many of the people planted their mealies twice, only to see their crops shoot up and wither away. As there was a scarcity of mealies throughout the colony the Government appealed to farmers and those with land to grow as much food as possible in preparation for the critical period which would occur between the end of the year and harvest time in May. The meal ration was allocated once a month and it had to last out. Two missions near Ingwenya were compelled to close down for lack of meal and Ingwenya seriously considered doing likewise. There were days when there just was no mealie meal – with, as Mfundisi put it, "one hundred and fifty hungry girls on the doorstep" – but the Mission managed to keep going.

Behind such a statement lay much anxiety and suffering. Wrote Jean, "The Government inspectors, Mr Stewart and Miss Rudd, spent two days here examining the school about four weeks ago. Among other recommendations they suggested that the children below Standard 1, of whom there are about 140, should be sent home at 11 am instead of at 1.30 pm as at present. These children, day-scholars, begin school at 7.30 am without any breakfast and have no food until they return to their homes at 2.30 pm or even later. The inspectors consider this too long a fast, as do we all, especially in these days of meagre meals. The little ones will not admit that they are hungry but on every occasion that the teacher's back is turned they can be heard crunching sugarcane behind their slates."

One evening towards the end of the year rain fell, a beautiful bountiful downpour that lasted nearly three hours. James Fraser was in the Nicolsons' house when the first drops were heard and all three rushed to the verandah and simply enjoyed it! They then filled as many baths and buckets as they could find. That was only a preliminary token. Jean described a later downpour: "It rained continuously for 28 hours and the rivers, usually mere sand tracks, were swollen and impassable and could be heard roaring over a mile away. An incident occurred recently on the road to Bembesi which may illustrate how the people feel about the rain. It was coming down in torrents and the car overtook a middle-aged man who was dripping from head to foot. To our surprise we found, as we glanced back at him in passing, that he was laughing to himself with sheer joy at being out in the rain!" One week in spring the school had to be closed for two days owing to the heavy rains. The women were soon out in their fields. Because their oxen had died many had great difficulty ploughing their land but the worst was over, for now.

The full reality of war was felt on the Mission one dark day when word came that Mackinlay's ship, a Swedish vessel on which he was returning to Scotland in order to enlist, had gone down with no survivors. That was all; no further news.

At this time of great sorrow words from a sermon preached by Rev Neil Cameron were much in Mrs Nicolson's mind. In her diary she had noted: "His text was, 'The Lord thy God will circumcise thy heart, and the heart of thy seed, to love the Lord thy God with all thy heart and with all thy soul that thou mayest live.' He said, 'If the Lord has circumcised your heart you will be saying, What about my son, and what about my daughter? But they are included in this promise. Bring them to the Lord at a throne of grace.'"

Several weeks later Mrs Nicolson received a letter requesting her to go to Cape Town. She went. There she was given details of a pension that was to be collected every month. It was such cold news to take back to Jean. She said, "I don't want to use it," and they never did collect the money.

During these years Jean also received the sad news that her close friend from school and university days, Mary Gatherar, had died in April 1942.

The Rev James Macleod, Greenock (1883-1963), who was a member of the Foreign Missions Committee for many years.

The teachers required close supervision and guidance so most evenings were taken up with corrections and helping the teachers with preparation. The teachers formed a community of their own. Most of them stayed on the Mission and some were married with families. They got on well together and were, in Jean's opinion, all capable teachers – some very enthusiastic! Each afternoon they met in one of the classrooms to plan the following day's work, look up textbooks, find illustrations, prepare lessons. Jean was at hand to guide them, make suggestions – in effect to continue their training, as necessary. This dedication on her part paid off. The benefit was apparent at every level in the school and no doubt it contributed to the high reputation in which Ingwenya School was held.

It will be appreciated that this support was necessary when it is realised that these teachers, with the highest qualifications to which they could aspire, were academically at the then level of First-Year secondary education in Scotland. After leaving school at Standard 6 they had done a further two years of study, including teacher training. When the opportunity arose to upgrade their qualifications by correspondence Jean helped them with English and arithmetic, and Doctor with hygiene. On obtaining their Junior Certificate, some with distinction, they received a well-deserved increase in salary.

The average African home at that time had no books and the teachers simply could not afford to buy any. To a plea in the *Free Presbyterian Magazine* for books and magazines of general interest there was a ready response. Two much-appreciated parcels of illustrated magazines arrived from New Zealand with the Prime Minister's compliments! A set of the *Children's Encyclopaedia* was among the books and posters that subsequently formed the nucleus of a Teachers' Resource Centre.

The Department was rethinking the syllabus, especially for Standards 5 and 6. Was it sensible to teach girls the intricacies of simple interest, decimals or cubic measurement, they wondered. Would some of the time not be better spent on First Aid and Child Welfare? And so it was decided.

Child Welfare was popular. Mrs Matola taught the girls how to look after a baby right from day one. Jean wrote that in most homes, "it's the old women, the Grannies, who take charge of these matters and they have very decided views of their own. Among other things the girls are told of a few safe medicines to use and warned that, contrary to popular opinion, teething powders do not produce teeth!

"Of the simplest rules of home-nursing the girls seem to know nothing and the sight of anyone of themselves in a faint is sufficient to produce hysterical screams. The lessons taught are of the simplest and most practical kind: that the patient should be kept quiet and not shaken when unconscious in an endeavour to bring him to his senses; that bathing in stagnant river pools may result in the painful and distressing bilharzia from which so many of them suffer; that pools and damp soil breed mosquitoes; that secondhand clothing should be boiled before being worn."

As part of their Industrial training the boys were building a new wash-house which did wonders for the girls' perception of Laundry as a school subject. Most, after two years' training in school, became excellent laundresses and could launder anything from a starched tablecloth to a man's linen suit.

It was teaching at its most rewarding. Shortages, improvising, crowding, though frustrating, can all be tolerated; there is even a certain satisfaction in making do and adapting. The great boon, and one which outweighed a thousandfold the inadequacies, was the fact of willing pupils with fresh young minds, eager to learn. The knowledge that one was making a difference to their potential for a worthwhile and satisfactory life was deeply satisfying. There was little in the way of discipline problems. What the youngsters desired was good teaching and if they got that they were delighted.

They worked hard, for in most cases they knew all too well that their education entailed sacrifices on the part of their parents. Final exams were held in November; results were awaited with considerable apprehension and generally received with relief or even glad surprise. A few pupils had to be told that they must repeat a class and there was much weeping and wailing as they pleaded to be allowed to go on, with promises to work really hard, while the headmistress pointed out that in the long run it would turn out for the better this way; some had simply missed too much school and in any case the decision had been taken by the Department, not by her.

Boarders leaving for the school holidays, their belongings "in a large roll . . . singing all the way".

After prize-giving they would receive their report cards and next morning set off at daybreak across the veldt, belongings in a large roll on head, singing all the way. World over there's no place like home!

Of those leaving school, six or seven would go to Teacher Training, some teach in out-schools and yet others become nurses or work in town before marrying and returning to the Reserve. There were those who married straight after school and acted as salt and leaven in the communities in which they set up home. The girls left at various stages, not all – in fact very few – staying the whole course to Standard 6.

On Prize-giving Day in November 1943, the school met to say goodbye to Paul Hlazo, who had taught there since 1925. He and his brothers had bought three adjoining farms about 300 miles from Ingwenya and the Government now decreed that all who owned farms must live on them, so he had to go. He was presented with a fur rug from the teachers and a money gift from the community. There were speeches expressing appreciation of his many years of conscientious work. In acknowledgment Paul recalled his boyhood days. "'Ingwenya will one day be a big school with European teachers and fine buildings,' my uncle promised. We thought he was joking! But – here we are! We have missionaries from Scotland with us and soon we'll have the buildings too. I hope you will go on at Ingwenya as you always have in the matter of education, putting the gospel and Christian living above all else."

Paul had been Mr Tallach's first interpreter. He recalled, "Paul was feeling his way at the new job and had not much fire then. Later on he entered more into the thought and feeling of what was being expressed and at times came almost to be an exact likeness of the speaker, right down to his tone and gesture.

"There are two kinds of interpreter. One translates quite literally, word for word, that which is spoken. This is not the best kind of interpreter, however. A good interpreter is careful to give the complete thought rather than the actual words and it is to this class that Paul belongs. Often when he knew that people were unable to follow the trend of a sermon through a literal translation of the words, by a slight movement of his hand he would indicate a pause until he had explained the matter more fully. Then by some apt illustration of his own he proceeded to clear up the matter. However good an interpreter may be, however, there is nothing to hold the attention of hearers like the direct address of the speaker. This holds true even when one's knowledge of a language is limited."

Stephen Hlazo, he who had met Mr Radasi on his first arrival, also had to move. He bought ground at Kwekwe where he built up a good congregation. One of his two sons, Harris, described as intelligent, bright and free from guile, died as a young man and a Christian. Stephen's other son, Cecil, was converted at Hope Fountain through the ministry of James Fraser. The Hlazo family, associated with the Mission since its inception, would be greatly missed both in school and church.

The spring of that year saw the death of MaHlabangana, one of Lobengula's five chief wives, a slight little woman but with tremendous authority. Back in 1914 she had professed Christianity. Most of her friends and relatives were connected to Lobengula and in old age she circulated among them, staying a few weeks here and a month or two there. They felt honoured to have her and acceded to her request, or rather demand, that a preacher be received from Ingwenya and the gospel was thus introduced to many a kraal. She did not hesitate to check wrongdoing where she saw it but Mr Tallach noticed that she never spoke of a person's faults except to the person himself, sternly perhaps but with a kindly twinkle. A few years before her death she attended the funeral of a grandson of Lobengula in East London on the shores of the Indian Ocean. On her return Mfundisi asked her, "And what, MaHlabangana, was the most wonderful thing you saw there?" Without hesitation she replied, "The sea. Oh, the wonderful sea! It stretched so far, far away before me and yet it was always coming towards me – it was like God's mercy, without measure."

The system of dotting kraals here and there was wasteful of land. In an attempt to remedy the situation or at least keep it from getting worse, the Government promoted the idea of building kraals in straight lines so that there would be virtually a long street of them instead of the more natural and picturesque arrangement to which the people were accustomed. The idea was to conserve pasturage for cattle and crops. Though they were not enamoured of the idea several such Lines had been built in the Reserve, one not far from Ingwenya. The women had many misgivings. What if their hens laid their eggs in the yard next door? How were they to know whether their next-door neighbour was a witch-doctor or not? They joked that the Europeans wanted them all together so that they could kill them all in one fell swoop.

Jean sometimes took an afternoon walk to the Line which lay to the west of the Mission. From the Mission gate, flanked by white-washed pillars, a track led to a small stream and continued across it to the Line, while another track branched north-west to the forest territory of Shangani. At its nearest end the Line was about a mile off and stretched for two miles – but in time it extended to six miles. There she visited the children in their homes, bringing gifts of food to the sick and needy.

To relieve overcrowding, a school was built at the Line for Beginners and Standard 1. It was an attractive T-shaped building with two rooms, each with four large windows and a fireplace for chilly winter days. Colourful pictures graced the whitewashed walls and long rows of smoothly plastered clay seats awaited their occupants. Jean wrote of the joy of seeing on opening day 90 neat little children "'with shining morning face' march smartly into school. This year we had to turn away about 20 little six-year-olds. We felt vexed to disappoint them and could not help admiring the anxious mother-care that lay behind their pretty pink dresses and khaki suits." Jean was to have oversight of this school, visiting it once or twice a week.

The accommodation problem at Ingwenya was somewhat eased but it was becoming obvious that the school situation required some radical thinking.. The academic success of Ingwenya School meant that the numbers applying for admittance far exceeded the capacity of the school. For some years students who had failed to get boarding places had been staying with local families and attending as day pupils, so much did they value education.

Mr Tallach spelled out the situation to the Synod. They had reached a crossroads. There were 13 teachers and 13 classes but only eight classrooms so that two classes had to be accommodated in the dining-room (with what inconvenience could be imagined), two in the church and one in a dormitory. And still the classrooms were as congested as ever – in spite of the schoolboys themselves building two school-rooms.

The Inspectors' attitude to the work at Ingwenya was most sympathetic. They understood the difficulties under which the school operated and had always been helpful. In 1944 an Inspector, Mr James Stewart, reported, "Our visit has assured us that the high standard which has characterised the school at Ingwenya for several years is being maintained. This applies both to academic and industrial subjects." He went on to make certain recommendations.

The appointment of an additional European teacher should be a priority. "The burden which Miss Nicolson carries is excessive. She is herself a full-time teacher of academic subjects and is, in addition, expected to supervise the work of all the other teachers both in academic and industrial subjects. . . . It is a physical impossibility to give the necessary supervision to the rest of the school while being at the same time responsible for a particular class."

Secondly, the erection of more classrooms was advisable. "We would suggest that your Committee consider the erection of a complete new school block. This is undoubtedly a tall order but we feel justified in making the recommendation since the present buildings were not apparently intended to be permanent and it would therefore, ultimately, be more economical to erect a permanent new school block than to continue erecting odd classrooms of a semi-permanent nature. . . . "

In the third place the provision of water for the girls' vegetable garden should receive attention. The present water supply was limited and too far away from the garden; much time was wasted carrying water from the well. The idea would be to have a large brick or concrete tank in the centre of the garden and to convey water to it by mechanical means.

The first two recommendations the home Church agreed to when conditions would allow and they advertised for a teacher, preferably male. Mfundisi and Doctor went about implementing the last suggestion by their own efforts and largely at their own expense.

With numbers just under 600, of whom 170 were boarders, the need for new buildings was urgent. An extensive building programme was envisaged including school premises, dormitory accommodation and in time a larger church. The time of coping by *ad hoc* measures was over. Jean expressed her pleasure at the prospect of a new school: "Dr Macdonald drew up a plan for a building shaped like the letter H, having six classrooms on either side and a common-room and office running across. A site has been

Ingwenya School showing one block – the other faced this.

A HEART FOR AFRICA

Ingwenya Mission beyond the River Jigijani.

chosen, subject to the Native Commissioner's approval, just outside the Mission fence. It is a pleasant park-like situation facing the west, near a gum-tree plantation. The ground slopes down to the Jigijani River and rises again on the other side towards the Line."

The project was supervised initially by the versatile Dr Macdonald and then by a builder from Glasgow, Mr Alexander McPherson, who arrived in April 1947. Doctor meanwhile valiantly went ahead as materials became available and against many obstacles; rain destroyed some bricks; then there was drought; cement was difficult to come by and expensive. He wrote, "In the past Ingwenya has earned a position as one of the best schools in the country . . . in spite of the fact that it has been one of the most poorly housed and equipped. Credit for this must be given to those who so devotedly laboured under most difficult conditions with inferior apparatus. We are now in process of remedying the most pressing defect in that we are engaged in erecting the first part of the new school."

The expansion of the school was driven by the hunger of the people for education but still the focus was on the preaching of the gospel. This was a Scottish Mission and as John Knox had given education a high priority in order that people could read the Word for themselves so it was at Ingwenya.

The Ntabazinduna Reserve was becoming overcrowded and people were being moved elsewhere, many to the Shangani Reserve, a huge area – much larger than the Ntabazinduna Reserve. Among them were some from Ingwenya including several of the leading men and elders. This left Ingwenya church rather depleted but seven young men were receiving instruction with a view to being ordained elders. At Zenka, in the depths of the Shangani forest, a church and a school had been established thanks to the evangelising efforts of John Mpofu and his son, Alexander. So much opposition had they encountered in the first years that Alexander had requested to be relieved of his post but Mr Tallach had persuaded him to hold on. Twelve years later he was able to say, "I am continually thankful that you persuaded me to stay on here and that the Lord gave me strength to do so. Not for all the money in the world would I have missed seeing the change which has come over the people through the

Mrs Jessie Nicolson and Mr John Mpofu (elder) outside the Nicolson's house.

A HEART FOR AFRICA

Jean Nicolson (back right) at a kraal school.

A class outside Ingwenya Primary School.

Approaching Ingwenya Mission.

Waiting at a bore hole.

A class at John Tallach Secondary School.

Primary School children.

Ready for a meal at John Tallach School.

Sports prize winners.

Leaving Ingwenya Mission.

Outside Mbuma Hospital.

Outside Nkai church in 1968.

Inside Ingwenya church.

John Tallach Secondary School.

Drying washing at a girl's dormitory in Ingwenya.

MaDonsa (grand-daughter of Lobengula, last king of the Matabele) and Esther, his great grand-daughter, whom she brought up.

Jean Nicolson in retirement.

Post-war Mission staff showing Mrs Jessie Nicolson front left, Jane Mackay in the centre and Mr Alexander McPherson on right.

Post-war Mission staff. Standing, left to right: Mrs Macdonald, Mrs Nicolson, Mrs Tallach, Mr Stewart, Inspector of Schools, Mr N Miller, Rev J Tallach, Catherine Tallach, Miss Nicolson, James Tallach. Sitting: Ian Tallach, Duncan Macdonald, Donny Macdonald, Margaret Tallach, Helen Tallach, Alasdair Macdonald, Ian Macdonald.

gospel and the school. More than that, I have a good hope of meeting in heaven some of my pupils, who were blessed by my Bible teaching in school." The people in Shangani were anxious to have a European missionary, expressly stating their preference that he would belong to the Free Presbyterian Church.

The War in Europe ended on 8 May 1945 and great was the rejoicing, muted by sorrow for the great loss of life and the suffering still being endured, for Japan did not surrender till August. Nevertheless VE Day was a day of thanksgiving though Jean and her mother felt sharply their particular loss.

Mr Tallach, Dr Macdonald and Jean were all overdue leave, but what with demobilisation and the continuing war in the East, there was little prospect of a sailing in the near future. James Fraser went home in September having been accepted as a student for the ministry and with the hope of returning to Rhodesia to carry on work already begun in the vast Shangani Reserve.

In December 1945 Norman Miller, who was stationed with the Forces in Kenya, made the long journey to Ingwenya. It was a significant visit for he subsequently joined the Mission.

Jane Mackay, a native of Staffin in Skye and a teacher in Portree High School, arrived in January after the heaviest downpour of the rainy season. Mr Tallach, Doctor and Jean set out to meet her and since the Ingwenya and Bembesi rivers were in flood they decided to cross country to avoid them. Jean described their journey; "We left Ingwenya about 6 am and soon encountered swollen streams and flooded fields. Suffice it to say that on three occasions oxen were sent for to tow the car and on many more occasions every available man was called upon to push the car through sheets of water. After four hours' struggle we had gone seven miles." Typical wet-season travel!

Everyone was keen to hear about the war. The teachers felt involved for they and others had contributed enthusiastically to the Feed Britain Fund, a pleasing exercise in mutual support and an opportunity to be benefactors. Jane, for her part, expressed herself as absolutely amazed at all that Jean had accomplished. She felt at home in no time and proved a capable and enthusiastic teacher.

By April Rev Edwin Radasi was back on African soil after an absence of 14 years, his return delayed because of the war. He went to Zenka, where he was to work with Paul Hlazo who had recently been appointed Head of the school.

In August the Tallach family set off for Scotland after 13 years in the field. Mr Tallach's health was giving cause for concern and in 1946 he resigned from the Mission. He had done heroically in establishing and expanding the work begun so manfully by Mr Radasi. Blessed with many gifts, he had by his writing and speaking fired the imagination of the people at home, young and old, with a vision of what could be accomplished by a few doing with their might what their hand found to do. He was called to the west-coast town of Oban, where he exercised a greatly-valued ministry.

One month later it was the turn of Jean and her mother to say good-bye. The years had seen a great expansion of the work and it was on the verge of a new era. Ingwenya School, through her efforts and those of Mr Fraser, now enjoyed an excellent reputation and continued to be held in high regard. The growing stage of the school was over. It was now to become a permanent institution. In general that period was also one of growth in the church with many new members being accepted.

Mrs Nicolson and Jean travelled to Cape Town where they were to board the *Caernarvon Castle*.

•

There was a sequel to the story of Mrs Nicolson's adventures at sea. Here it is as remembered by Jean:

Mother and I were going home on a long-delayed furlough. During these years we had had the heart-breaking news of the disappearance of the ship on which Mackinlay had hoped to reach England. Mother had had a fall at Ingwenya and had broken a hip. Dr Macdonald was there but she wouldn't have any treatment. She was very upset because we had lost my brother and she didn't want any sympathy. So she was quite lame by the time we arrived in Cape Town and boarded the *Caernarvon Castle*. It was still Troop Deck as it had been when carrying troops. Mother was in a cabin for twenty as she was over 60. I was in a cabin – or dormitory, I should say – for over ninety. Like everyone else I queued, with my two trays, for every meal. One afternoon Mother hobbled up to me as I stood in the queue for afternoon tea while she sat in the lounge.

"Do you see that bald man, three in front of you?"

"Yes," I said.

"That is the Jew I put out of the cabin," said Mother.

"Oh nonsense, Mother!" I said. "Go and sit down!"

"No; I am going to speak to him."

"How can you speak to him after the way you treated him?"

"Yes, I'm going to speak to him," she insisted and went and stood beside him. "Excuse me, were you on the *Gao Bello* in 1940?"

"Yes. What do you know about that?"

"I am the lady that put you out of the cabin."

"Oh, how are you?" he said shaking hands warmly.

"I'm well, but how is your wife?" Mother asked.

"She is well. We are not two now. We are four!"

An extraordinary meeting after six years!

● C H A P T E R   1 1 ●

Troubled Years

A T home the scene was one of desolation. The Nicolsons were aghast at the bomb damage. Jagged buildings were standing on derelict ground and rubble-strewn tracts of land awaited clearing. Rationing was still in force and, though basic commodities were adequate, many goods were unobtainable or in short supply. But the war was over.

In the church in Glasgow Rev D J Matheson was soon to be inducted. Their friend, Rev Roderick Mackenzie had resigned amid controversy and the congregation was just settling down again after the turmoil so it was not altogether an easy homecoming.

Mrs Nicolson's health concerns put any thought of a return to the Mission out of the question meantime and in any case the Church was advertising for a headmaster for Ingwenya. After visiting Lochinver, where they rented a cottage, they spent some time in Glasgow and in May they moved to Strathaven for Jean had obtained a post in the nearby village of Stonehouse.

It was to their stay in Glasgow that Jean later traced the first appearance of "the thread of desire to return to Africa". She felt so strong and fit and wondered why she should have such health and energy – surely not to be expended on an easy or self-indulgent life? "I remember," she told her journal, "praying definitely one weekend that I'd get some encouragement in St Jude's if it were the will of the

Most High that I should return. Mr Matheson that evening spoke in a way remarkably suitable to my prayer when he dwelt on the spirit possessed by the Apostle Paul, when he counted not his life dear unto himself but gloried in the cross of Christ, by whom the world was crucified unto him and he unto the world."

In Strathaven they had "some months of peace and quiet to read and study" and enjoyed the company of the friends they made there among the Brethren. One of these friends lent them the *Life of Colliard,* which Jean describes as "a most fascinating book which fired my desire and possibly Mother's too to return to Africa." The morning reading for 30 August in Spurgeon's *Morning and Evening* readings spoke to them in the same tenor. The following October, when they were at church in Greenock, the minister, Rev James Macleod asked her, "When are you going to Africa? The post is yours." Apparently there had been no application for the post of headteacher. So Jean left Stonehouse at the end of January 1948. It had been "an easy post but not as absorbing as work in Africa."

She lost no time in going to Thomas Cook's to inquire about a passage to South Africa. As she discussed options and possibilities with the booking clerk she became aware of a lady making travel arrangements at another counter and caught the word, "Canada".

"Very good, Miss Nicolson. We'll contact you as soon as we have firm information," concluded the clerk.

"Thank you," said Jean.

Then she heard herself say, "And now would you please tell me about sailings to New York? For three, please."

Next morning she was offered three berths on the *Queen Elizabeth,* sailing to New York on 20 March. Aunt Johan was going too. Mrs Gatherar made it a quartet.

Jean wrote of their travels in her journal. One entry bears out her contention that one could always pick out the missionaries on board ship: "We got in touch with no Christians on board until one afternoon a party of us was being shown around the first class. As we surged up the stairs at one point, a stream of people passed down. Out of the corner of my eye I noticed someone different from the others.

'I'm sure that's a missionary,' I whispered. The lady smiled.

'Are you a missionary?' I asked.

'Yes. Are you?'

'Yes. Where?'

'South America. Where are you?'

'Southern Rhodesia.' We passed on."

From New York, where they found the "briskness and speed exhilarating", they went by train to Toronto and on to Winnipeg. In both these places they had the pleasure of meeting Ingwenya Support groups. They visited Mrs Nicolson's brothers and their families and Jean's warm affection for them shines through: "Our very dear Bubo, pale and thin but with the same charm of manner, and Dorothy, so sweet and self-effacing; Uncle Dan, stooped but well and happy-looking, and Margaret who hadn't been sleeping well; Don with his many and varied interests and Miriam who did everything she could to make us happy. At Glaslyn it made us sad to see the old store where Uncle Bill and family worked and lived for so many years."

At Regina they parted with Mrs Gatherar. There they were entertained by a Mountie friend, "magnificently tall in his fur cap", who showed them round town, and drove them to the stables to meet his horse! Another special memory for Jean was the thrill of climbing – by chair-lift – to a mountain-top from where they had "a wonderful view of a thousand peaks glittering in the afternoon sun."

They flew from Nelson to Calgary, perhaps their first flight. Some 20 passengers were on the CPA plane which "rose like a bird and circled round the peaks of the mountains bordering the valley, revealing silver streams, rivers and cliffs in an ever-widening circle until we rose to 8,000 or 9,000 feet. Crossing the valleys, the plane dipped and pulled downwards but otherwise the flight was smooth and the scenery magnificent." They touched down for lunch and took to the air again "right over the clouds. Occasionally there was a chink, and we could see far below us streams and valleys. At times, especially before rising to a greater height, the plane seemed to hover for a few seconds as it balanced from wing to wing and one momentarily held one's breath." Further miles over the "flat and dreary prairies" and they were there!

Towards the end of May they left New York on the *Queen Mary* for a few weeks in Scotland with their minds reaching on toward

A group at Mbuma in 1958.
Left to right: Ma Ngwenya (very tall and a church member at Zenka), MaZwabo (very short) in front, Rev James Fraser, Miss Finlayson (Mr Fraser's sister-in-law) and John Mpofu.

Africa. In July Jean and her mother sailed on the *Stirling Castle* for Cape Town for what promised to be a time of expansion and coming-of-age for the school at Ingwenya.

Jane Mackay had admirably kept the work going. A conscientious, lively and enthusiastic teacher with a bright personality she had reported encouragingly about the school, so Jean was looking forward to a third spell of hard but rewarding work.

The Tallach family, such a constant of days past, were greatly missed but it was good to have Doctor and Mrs Macdonald and their family of four boys still there. James Fraser with his wife and baby Elizabeth had arrived the previous September. They and Edwin Radasi were settled at Zenka in the Shangani Reserve.

Ingwenya was quite transformed. Under Mr McPherson's direction an extensive building operation was under way with some buildings already up and in use, so the compound offered a scene of purposeful activity. It would be 1952 before the whole programme would be completed, by which time there would be two blocks of six classrooms, four girls' dormitories, a sanitary block for the girls, a dining-room, a house for the Matron and houses for staff living on the Mission. Sometimes the opportunity was taken to involve the pupils. When ten boys from Zenka were received as boarders, they built their own dormitory and a small dining-room as part of their education.

The new buildings were a pleasure to work in. Jane described a typical classroom as having a splendid wall blackboard, running the whole breadth of the room, and on the opposite wall a smaller blackboard with a map on each side. Every room had a cupboard and a table and some even boasted a chair! Doctor had designed and constructed, with the help of a local joiner, very good substantial desks. "No one, but one who has attempted to teach in entirely different circumstances, can fully appreciate the joy of teaching in our new classrooms."

But what Jean and her mother noticed most was the blank left by the departure of men who had been the backbone of the congregation at Ingwenya – men like John Dabengwa, John Mthamo, Stephen Mntambo and the brothers Hlazo, who had bought farms elsewhere and gathered a nucleus of worshippers around them. Some, including Philemon Ndebele, had moved to Zenka and other parts of Shangani. Old Isaiah Nyati had died. Patrick Mzamo's wife was among the godly women who had passed away. The remaining members from the early days, like Amos Ngombane, were old now.

Rev A B Ndbele, Mr Philemon Ndebele (father), Mrs Philemon Ndebele (mother) and Mrs A B Ndebele

Isaiah Nyati, lithe and full of enthusiasm, had been raised in heathenism. He had come to Mr Radasi's church after being for a time with the Wesleyans and eventually was ordained an elder at Ingwenya. In 1927 he moved to Gwisani, at that time quite a backward area, and soon gathered a congregation. As befitted a warrior who had fought in one of Lobengula's crack regiments he could say with truth, "I fear no man. My only fear is that men will not fear me!"

In 1940 Mr Tallach went to Gwisani to conduct communion services and found a roomy new church. On enquiring who had built it he was told that Isaiah and his wife MaKumalo had done most of the work themselves. He was astonished. "How they managed the roof is a mystery and then the thatching! He must be 70 years old and his wife 60. He is like no other person. As a preacher he is very apt and commands great attention."

On the Monday of that weekend Isaiah addressed the people, "I got in that text yesterday what has filled me right up. I feel so full of this wonderful truth about the blood of Jesus cleansing us of all sin that you may expect me to preach on it next Sabbath and the next and the next!"

After his death in 1947 one of the elders said, "Isaiah Nyati always said that he wished to die clinging to Christ and he is blessed in that he did die clinging to Christ." He was survived by his wife, a wise and gracious woman, and seven children.

Another member of longstanding was MaMlotshwa, grandmother of Esther Donsa who had been a pupil at Ingwenya in Mr Tallach's early years. A tall handsome woman, imperious in manner, she had in her heathen days been much given to fighting and wild behaviour especially when drunk. One afternoon on her way to a beer drink her attention was caught by a small crowd gathered round the elder, John Dabengwa. Curiosity impelled her to approach within listening distance and she heard the gospel for the first time. Whenever she saw similar groups she joined them and then started going to church. When she was converted the change in her life was obvious to all.

In a letter to a friend in Scotland Jean expresses her affection for these old friends; "Jane, Mr Radasi and I were at a Parents' Meeting at Libeni three miles from here on Saturday afternoon. On the way back we stopped at the village of a dear old lady, MaMlotshwa. She is getting very frail but is so bright and always in church until the last few weeks, when her poor old back has begun to ache. She was one of the chief wives of the last king and gets a pension. But she has a stream of hangers-on who eat up all her money. She complained of toothache. Just before Doctor went off we went to see her. She pointed to a tooth that was troubling her. Doctor pretended to feel if it was loose – when whisk out it came! I felt like doing the same but was afraid I mightn't be successful. One feels sad to see the dear old folk fading away. Another old man Nombembe at Bembesi is getting very weak. Last time we were there he asked me to name all Mr Tallach's family and went over them, counting on his fingers. He wanted Mr Tallach and Doctor to know how ill he was. . . . The old grannies are the most faithful at attending the prayer meeting. One old dear came up to Jane and me and said she wanted a medicine to make her blood go round and round very fast through her body – it didn't seem to be moving at all! She has recently become a member. I may have told you about her before. She asked the kirk session to give her a new name as she had been such a great sinner while having her present one."

MaMlotshwa died not very long afterwards. Her last words were, "Receive Thou me, Oh Lord of Glory!"

The people were clamouring for education. Parents were willing to make sacrifices to have their children educated and the school was more crowded than ever with 16 teachers and around 500 pupils at Ingwenya, while in the Line School three teachers taught over 100 little ones. Ten teachers lived on the Mission. More and more children were starting school at age six and, while it was still the case that they left at various stages, the numbers staying on till Standard 6 had dramatically increased.

Jean asked herself the question, How great a part should education play in the work of the Mission? The three chief aims of the educational work as she saw it were firstly the conversion of the children; secondly the training of those of more than average ability and character as leaders and moulders of public opinion and thirdly the raising of the general population to a better standard of living. This last was being achieved indirectly through educational and medical provision. The second was being frustrated by the fact that able youngsters were often unable to proceed farther than primary school; secondary schools had long waiting lists and Missions gave priority to their own young people. One of the inspectors had suggested that the solution lay in opening a secondary school at Ingwenya. As for the first aim, while there were many who seemed scarcely touched by the gospel, others were living genuine Christian lives. These are the underlying motives that informed her approach to teaching.

One aspect of the Mission was all too familiar as her correspondence reveals; "What worries us most these days are donkeys and goats. The Reserve is as bare as a board, not a blade of grass after three years of drought and the animals are desperate with hunger. They push through barbed wire and thorns and come in by hook or by crook foraging for scraps. Not long ago I heard a terrible crash at our wooden gate, then another and another. It was 11 pm and pitch dark. I ran over, torch in hand, and here was a donkey caught between the wooden bars of the gate. He couldn't go in or come out and had kicked the gate to pieces.

"On Sabbath night we were just settling down to worship when the girls could be heard screaming with excitement. I went over to see and here they were belabouring a few poor donkeys which refused to budge. Having reproached them for making such a noise I had just arrived home when there were more screams, of alarm this time. I ran and here they were belabouring a snake which had been making its way into a dormitory. I commended them on this occasion as usually they are too scared to do anything but run for assistance."

Snakes were a continuing hazard. Doctor and James Fraser had gone to Gwatemba about 80 miles distant to keep services and there they had, as Doctor put it, "one of those little experiences which give a certain zest to missionary work. As the weather was very hot we decided not to sleep in the hut put at our disposal so we placed our camp beds outside, up against the front of the car. Before going off to sleep we discussed the wonderful African sky above our heads, when Mr Fraser remarked on some peculiar noise near his head, then sat up very quickly with the words, 'It's a snake!' It cannot be a pleasant feeling to have a snake make its way across one's neck! After a fruitless hunt for the disturber of our peace who were soon asleep under the stars. The following day the people gathered in the chief building on the farm, a large round hut. Sitting on an old settee and chairs of various designs round a large table, a small company met to commemorate the love of the Saviour, dear to all who know Him."

Dr Macdonald and his family sailed for Scotland in late 1948 for the last time after an 11-year term. Realising that in places near towns there would soon be no need for medical missions he resigned from the Mission field after 20 years' service. It was a link with the early days gone. He had thoughts about writing an account of the work done by Rev John Tallach but a busy pastorate probably precluded that for in January 1951 he was inducted to the charge of Vancouver in Canada where he was a much-loved pastor.

Jean now became superintendent of the secular side of the work in addition to her existing responsibilities. While Jane and Jean each had her own class, Jane's special remit was to supervise Ingwenya School and Jean's was the responsibility for the Line school and the seven kraal schools attached to Ingwenya. It had been the policy of the Mission to set up a kraal school only when a preaching station had been opened. Often the teacher and preacher were one and the same person though in other cases the church services were taken by an elder. It was impossible to keep pace with the demand for education – in spite of the contribution that parents were willing to make. They were expected to build the school, to see to any necessary repairs, to provide accommodation and food for teachers whose homes were not in the vicinity, to plough the school field and provide seed for it and to pay for all books used by their children. No charge was made for tuition.

Teachers were leaders. What they taught was expected to be of use in the community and, like it or not, they were by their very status regarded as examples. Most were Christians and in Mr Tallach's opinion their role was pivotal to the future of Africa. "For the teacher who goes to reside among heathen people and who patiently labours on, year after year until he sees a change come over them, I have the deepest sympathy and the highest respect. I look up to him as one of the finest products of the gospel and one of the greatest forces in the shaping of Africa's future."

Schools varied in size. Some were one-teacher schools, some larger. Some were pole and dagga, others were built of raw bricks and thatched. Some had desks, in others the pupils perched with slates on knees. All were simply equipped – blackboard, ruler and chalk, a table, chair and cupboard. Pupils sat on rude wooden benches or on long forms made of dried mud and rounded on top. Jean had drawn up schemes of work for each subject in each class, detailing week by week the work that might be covered in a year. She had also made flash-cards for arithmetic and reading – cards with words or number facts printed on them and used as an aid to memorising when the teacher held up a card and the class gave an immediate response: they could be used for matching name to object or for any purpose the teacher's ingenuity decreed.

The Department was now taking more interest in these schools. They were inspected regularly, grants were more generous and few had teachers with less than Standard 6 qualification while some even had certificated teachers. Sewing, basketry, gardening and agriculture had been added to the usual academic subjects. However, though there had been a general improvement standards were still regrettably low.

Each school had a committee which included at least two elders or deacons so the school was a real part of the Christian effort in the neighbourhood. An early prayer meeting was held each Thursday morning at which children and adults listened to a simple address. On Sabbath morning a prayer meeting was followed by Sabbath school. In the evening there was a Bible class for older children and adults.

Kraal schools must be visited and examined at least four times a year and Jean enjoyed her contact with them. She describes one such visit to Maqaqeni about three miles from Ingwenya. "Maqaqeni means among the hills and it is situated in the Fingo Location where the language is Xhosa, whereas Ingwenya is in the Matabele Reserve and the language is Ndebele. The little thatched school stands on a hill surrounded by mimosa thorn, at times aglow with yellow blossom. Not a person is to be seen on my arrival on a certain morning at 7.45 am. Having entered the classroom to see if the blackboard has been prepared, I notice that one of the walls has been rebuilt and the thatch repaired. This is gratifying. The children begin to arrive about 8 am and the young teacher, Ethel Nombembe, arrives too. She passed Standard 6 at Ingwenya in 1949 and this is her first post.

About 8.20 am the head teacher, Abia Sobantu, appeared. "Under his arm he carries his registers, and in his hand a bottle of ink and a basket of chalk. When we have greeted each other and I have enquired after his wife and three children, he apologises for being late; he has no time, he says, his time is broken, meaning his watch. However, my irritation at finding him late is dissipated as I hear him give a very pleasing Bible lesson on the trial of Abraham, punctuated by such questions as: Does God still try His people? Sometimes He tries them with hunger. There is no food in the fields. There is no rain. The people of the world say, 'He does not care,' but God's people say, 'He loves us still. He will take care of us.' Abraham praised God for providing a ram. Do you praise God for sending His Son? The Lord's people praise Him, for He died for their sins.

"Then the examination begins. We begin with the little ones and find that the little six-year-olds cannot read. 'They are refusing to learn,' says their teacher, looking at them anxiously, meaning that they have been unable to grasp anything. Having tested a little fellow called Umhlabobansi the world is wide I find it is even so. He knows nothing. So we proceed to the older children and find them anxious and eager to show off their learning. Having gone through the three Rs to Standard Two I ask if they can sing, and therewith little Abia Sobantu starts up the 40th Psalm and, as they sing very softly and sweetly in three parts, Abia conducts the singing, waving his arms with the greatest precision and solemnity.

"At 11 am we begin Industrial work. The girls have sewing and most of the pretty materials have come from Canada. Having tried on the garments and examined the stitchery I promise to send some more material. The boys are doing woodwork, [making] coat-hangers, ox-skeys and wooden spoons. All the school seats have been made by the boys. As I prepare to leave, three little fellows approach shyly and ask for a lift in the car. So, having consented, they scramble into the back of the little vanette and we all speed down the hill, through the little stream and up the other side, accompanied by screams of delight from the little boys."

That school was under an experienced teacher in contrast to a school opened shortly after at Induba Farm about nine miles from Ingwenya. The teacher there was a lad of 16 who had recently passed Standard 6 at Ingwenya. He also ran a night-school for parents who wished to learn how to read and write. Among the 22 pupils was a boy who was unable to walk, the legacy of an attack of infantile paralysis, and his father was the most eager of all that the school should prosper.

One fine April morning Jean and Jane set off for Nukwa, where lived the brothers Sithole. There was a certain sadness for it would probably be their last visit since the people were being moved in July. "After Miss Mackay and I had examined the classes Sithole offered to take us to a farm at no great distance, where the people were very anxious to open a school. We all got into the car and followed another cart track through fields and valleys and over river banks, which we got out to inspect many times before venturing to cross, while the little Austin groaned and reeled from one obstacle to the next. At last we emerged into a plain and as we neared a village a group of men, women and children darted towards the car, calling out the greeting, 'Salibonani!' The women seemed to be overjoyed and after shaking hands all round one woman kept dancing about, clapping her hands and saying to her little daughter over and over again, 'Now you will learn, now you will learn!'"

A highlight was a visit Jane and Jean paid to Makwiro 300 miles north of Ingwenya. They were met at the station by Cecil Hlazo who drove them to Stephen Hlazo's farm next to his own. This Stephen it was who had first noticed Mr Radasi at Bulawayo station long years before. Well-educated and knowledgeable he spoke entertainingly about those early days. He told how he hauled wood 90 miles in his own wagon to build the first church at Ingwenya and described vividly how in those early days the countryside around Ingwenya was thickly wooded and zebra and giraffe roamed free. Mrs Hlazo was as attractive as her husband. They had a most comfortable house, furnished European-style. The Fraser family had come from Zenka as Mr Fraser was to take the communion services. On Sabbath morning his text was, "Behold the Lamb of God!" and Jean noticed that at each point he made, one woman turned to her friend and stared hard at her as if to say, "Did you hear that?" As they were parting on Monday Stephen said that that Sabbath had been one of the happiest of his life.

An extensive Government programme for the treatment and prevention of tuberculosis was being put into effect and doctors duly arrived at Ingwenya. The health of the children in the district they considered above average and Jean told how they "commented on the sturdy way even the tiny tots, children of four and five, marched up to the doctors, extended small brown arms and received an injection without a whimper or a tear."

Jean's visit to Makwiro, with Stephen Hlazo (above) and Mrs Hlazo (below).

Before this there was little one could do to combat this disease. Georgina was a young girl of 12 who contracted tuberculosis and eventually became so ill that she could not leave her home. Her parents looked after her anxiously but for all their care she grew steadily weaker. Her father, who was a heathen, suggested consulting a witchdoctor but Georgina would not hear of it. Their kraal was not far from the church and whenever there was a service she would ask her parents to carry her outside so that she could listen to the singing of the

psalms. One day she told her mother that she wanted to be left alone as she would like to have a short time of prayer by herself. When her mother returned, Georgina said, "Mother, I'll soon be leaving you all but you must not cry for me. I'm going to a better land, a happy land and, Oh Mother, you must go on seeking Christ and you will go there too". Shortly afterwards she passed away. There was as yet no preventative injection for poliomyelitis.

One day a European farmer called. "One of my workers has a young daughter who's had infantile paralysis and she's in a wheelchair. I wonder if you would take her in as a boarder?" Rhoda was ten years old and proved to be bright and intelligent. She was very popular with the girls, almost as popular as her chair, so she was rarely the sole occupant! And, when the chair was out of commission, the girls vied with one another for the privilege of carrying her, piggy-back, all over the Mission.

A *Pilgrim's Progress* class for the boarders was held every Wednesday evening. They loved the story and enjoyed discussing the names – Mr Fearing, Mr Talkative, Mr Ready-to-Halt, Mrs Bat's Eyes – for some of which it was difficult to find equivalents in a different language. They had been told something of Bunyan's life and how his little blind daughter used to sit beside him in prison as he wrote his book. This gripped their imagination. To one small girl the whole story was so real that she asked, "Misi, do you know if the little blind girl arrived in the Celestial City too?"

Buildings and personnel were not the only differences Jean and her mother had noticed; there was something more subtle, a change of atmosphere, a general malaise. And they sensed a difference in attitude to them personally. The first stirrings of the "wind of change" that was to sweep Africa and other colonies worldwide, though it had yet to gain momentum, was making itself felt in Southern Rhodesia. Young men home from the War had expectations of a new world order as is not unnatural when men have fought bitterly to defend freedom. They had come into contact with new ideas and had seen conditions in a wider sphere. Immigrants from Britain were flooding into the country, their country! "Africa for the Africans!" was a powerful slogan.

This uprising of African nationalism was at first centred in the towns. In 1947 there took place the first ever strike of workers in

Bulawayo. It was Africans near the towns who were most affected by the dissension and turmoil and Nationalist aspirations tended to be strongest among the more educated. Among the teachers and office-bearers of the church at Ingwenya there were some who supported the growing movement.

In her teaching role and when visiting kraal schools Jean experienced the fall-out from this new suspicion of the white usurpers of their land, as some saw it, and for the first time she was aware of a certain undercurrent of resentment from some of the young male teachers. Part of the trouble was the absence of the old men and elders. The lack of their stabilising influence was crucial.

After Dr Macdonald's departure Edwin Radasi moved to Ingwenya to take over ministerial duties temporarily and Jean wrote appreciatively of "the pleasant way in which Mr Radasi has always been ready to help Miss Mackay and myself." But he was meeting secretly with young men who were now office-bearers, some of whom saw no reason why there need be white missionaries at all. When asked about the matter he did not deny it. Mr Fraser asked to see the minutes of these meetings; no minutes had been kept. Mr Radasi had complained to Jean that he was finding the office-bearers a hindrance rather than a help.

When Jane went on leave in January 1951 Jean must, by Government regulation, devote all her time to Ingwenya, so she handed oversight of the kraal schools to Mr Radasi. She had a heavy responsibility as superintendent of Ingwenya, head of a large boarding school and class teacher. The situation continued to deteriorate and the European staff wrote to the Committee in Scotland requesting that they send a deputation to make a thorough investigation.

Instead they sent out a young minister. In March 1951, newly-ordained, he arrived from Scotland with his wife to take over the pastoral oversight of Ingwenya congregation and was warmly received by the Mission staff. However, he was soon embroiled in trouble. Inexperienced as he was, he listened too readily to the disaffected Africans and a difficult situation only got worse as he went along with them.

The suspicion against the missionaries grew and, while Rev James Fraser had to defend himself from accusations of malpractice, it was the Nicolsons who were the central focus of mistrust and resentment. Scowls and suspicious looks were directed at them. Mr Radasi's wife would not speak to them. Things got so bad that Jean confided that she was grateful, almost to tears, if a child smiled at her. They were accused, silently at least, of using mission funds to enrich themselves. As someone remarked, eloquently and sufficiently, "Imagine! Mrs Nicolson! Jean!"

The minister was recalled, leaving after six months but he and his wife left a trail of unrest and trouble behind them. For two years Jean could not visit a home on the Line. The local people refused to acknowledge her or her mother and would ignore their greeting. It was a time to which she seldom referred and then only briefly but there is no doubt it was a most painful and distressing experience, one of the saddest of her life. To his credit, many years later the minister concerned called to see her when she had retired to Edinburgh and apologised for his behaviour – which apology she accepted.

Jean's vexation was not purely on her own account and her mother's. The assault came close to wrecking their credibility and undoing the work of years. She was the remaining representative, with James Fraser, of all that the Mission had stood for. If they were imposters, all that they had done and taught, together with James' present preaching, was undermined – and little wonder though the local people should be antagonistic. It was a blow at the whole work.

In this crisis Mr Fraser was a great support as were also some of Jean's long-serving teachers, notably Simon Moyo. Fortunately the trouble was confined to Ingwenya. It was a personal assault on the integrity of Jean and her mother and, though Jean was confident of being vindicated, the trial, while it lasted, was severe.

Mr Radasi and all but a few of the congregation left the Mission and set up a rival church. The staff received quite a shock when he left; it was all very sudden – a note saying he had gone! He was eventually deposed. It was sad to see him trying to break down what his father had so valiantly built up. Family loyalty played its part in the exodus while many of the local people were not unnaturally confused by the whole business. In ensuing years quite a number returned to the Mission, but it was a damaging split.

These troubles did not prevent the Mission staff from carrying out their normal duties to such effect that results in school maintained what had become their usual high standard. Norman Miller arrived to supervise the kraal schools while Mrs Miller and Mrs McPherson helped out in Zenka school. James Fraser had moved down to Ingwenya when the minister there was recalled and in August Jane returned. They heard that a second minister, newly-ordained, was on his way out to Africa.

After almost six tumultuous years Mrs Nicolson and Jean were ready for their much-needed leave. Jane was left in charge of the school in these most difficult circumstances. There had been a few months of relative calm but it would not last. Later in the year trouble broke out again, this time culminating in open rebellion among the older pupils. The second minister to come from Scotland was recalled after 18 months but the aftermath of these years of turmoil was not so easily dealt with.

Jean and her mother sailed for home in February 1954. The home Church sent an assurance of support to the European staff: "Having regard to the period of trouble and anxiety they have recently passed through, the time seems opportune for giving expression to the Synod's confidence in their faithfulness as missionaries and their conduct of all affairs connected with the Mission. The Synod is particularly happy to recall that this year Miss Nicolson completes 20 years' service. During those years the mission has progressed beyond recognition. The Synod gratefully recognises the part contributed by Miss Nicolson toward such development."

● CHAPTER 12 ●

John Tallach Secondary School

REV FINLAY MACLEOD and his wife were about to set off on a year's preaching tour in Australia and New Zealand and wrote to Mrs Nicolson offering her the use of their manse in Dornoch while home on leave. They were delighted and so had a very comfortable stay in this ancient and royal burgh in north-east Scotland. On the national scene a considerable rebuilding programme had largely restored a sense of normality and the young Queen Elizabeth had succeeded her father on the throne.

It was while they were in Scotland that they received news of the sudden death in October 1955 of Rev John Tallach. A large crowd of friends and townspeople attended his funeral in Oban. On hearing the news an African friend observed, "It can be said of Mr Tallach that he preached more by deed than by word. His life was a powerful sermon to many souls in Rhodesia".

Rev James Macleod said, "He was one of the most unselfish men we ever worked with, as if born and moulded for missionary work. Mrs Tallach shared the joys and worries of her husband ungrudgingly and silently all these years. She helped in many ways the women, girls and boys in the way that they should go, and by her own example impressed upon the mind of young and old that the Christian manner of living was the best and the noblest." Mrs Tallach outlived her husband by almost fifty years and despite the sorrow of

Mrs Jessie Nicolson, Jean and Miss MacAskill (Mrs Nicolson's sister) sitting in front of the Dornoch manse while on furlough in 1955.

seeing her two sons die before her she remained unfailingly cheerful, trusting in the goodness of God.

By January 1956 Jean and her mother were back at Ingwenya in time for the new session beginning at the end of that month. The words of Mark 13:34, "and to every man his work", had lodged in her mind till she felt compelled to return to the Mission.

Norman Miller, with his family, was there as Superintendent and Miss Mackay was delighted to have her old colleague back. Mr McPherson had resigned because of ill-health and, when he left with his wife and young son, his place was taken by James Tallach, son of Rev John Tallach. He had trained as a joiner but seemed able to turn his hand to anything and being fluent in Ndebele his services as interpreter were much in demand. The sentiment was voiced once and again, "Ingwenya seems to be complete now that the Nicolsons are back!"

With its new buildings the Mission was the picture of a well-cared-for and orderly environment. Trees and shrubs were tended, watered, and defended from marauding goats by pupils, enthusiastically wielding sticks, stones – or threats. Gardens were ablaze with red and purple bougainvillea, pink and white oleander and the fragrant frangipani shrub with its smooth bark and delicate cream and yellow scented flower.

Before school opened the Mission staff had the pleasure of entertaining Revs Donald MacLean and Robert Sinclair, whom the home Church had belatedly sent out as deputies. Arriving in January they stayed till April and were warmly welcomed throughout the Mission. It was a relief to have fresh eyes look at the situation and it was reassuring for the home Church to have a first-hand report; rumours of trouble and uncertain information had made some withdraw their support financially and in other ways – perhaps not unnaturally, for those with slender resources felt responsible for how they disposed of their money.

Things had settled down somewhat but tension remained. Numbers in the congregation were greatly depleted and it would be only slowly that some who had followed Mr Radasi would return. However, there were those who had come back and the atmosphere was happier and healthier than for some years.

Visiting Deputies, Revs D MacLean and R R Sinclair, with elders at Mbuma.

A HEART FOR AFRICA

The visiting ministers travelled extensively about the Mission on their fact-finding tour and at a meeting with the Inspectors at the Education Department they were given the opportunity of examining the annual reports. That for 1952 read; "Ingwenya Mission has produced the best results of the circuit, and the organisation and conduct of this school have been attended to most conscientiously." The next year's included, "Miss Nicolson takes with her the sincere appreciation of this Office for all she has done at Ingwenya." The most recent, for 1955, stated, "The internal organisation of the classroom work is in the capable hands of Miss Mackay. Despite the fact she has Standard 6 class to teach full-time, she is active in supervising teachers and classwork, and the general satisfactory level of the school work is a credit to her efforts." Miss Cornwall-Jones, Inspector, confirmed that Mrs Ncube, matron and teacher of Domestic Science was "a good and dependable person, her handwork excellent and her discipline good." They were told, "One headmaster judges how difficult an examination is by the results obtained by Ingwenya as the marking is considered to be so honest."

The clothes worn by these children were all made by pupils in the Domestic Science class at Ingwenya Mission

A former Director of Education remarked that one mission leaving a stamp on the people was Ingwenya.

Inspector Hodson wrote: "When I first came to know Ingwenya I realised at once that the cordial atmosphere that existed and the good academic work being done there were due almost entirely to the ability and personality of Miss Nicolson – and no small credit must also be given to Mrs Nicolson."

Before leaving in April the deputies made several useful suggestions. Water from the well was being stored in drums and used as required. However, Miss Nicolson's house had recently been provided with an internal water system – both hot and cold water and sanitation – and this amenity should be extended to other houses. Water from the well should be piped to the Mission for the benefit of teachers and boarders alike. House furnishings were provided by the staff themselves and only some had refrigerators but as these were essential in a hot climate they should be supplied out of Mission funds. Merely to anticipate such luxuries lifted one's spirits!

Jean's return coincided with the Government's new Five-Year Plan for Education. The whole system was to be overhauled and the

School boarders in 1965.

A HEART FOR AFRICA

educational programme was to be accelerated. In effect this was an attempt to regularise the education of African children. As things stood, few of those who did start school stayed beyond Standard 3. All children within reach of a school were now to be given five years of education. In order to weed out over-age pupils from the lower classes the pupils must now begin school between the ages of seven and ten instead of starting school at any age from six to 16. Any child who had not passed Standard 3 by 14 years of age might not proceed to Standard 4. Jean found that in practice this last prohibition meant that, as many parents just did not know the age of their older children, they simply became younger on the register year by year! So Ingwenya boasted some surprisingly mature eight-year-olds!

To implement the Plan many more teachers would be required. The Government therefore proposed establishing new Secondary Schools and Teacher Training establishments and promised generous financial help to any Mission willing to do likewise. The Government regarded Christian missions with favour, not only for their educational input but also for their spiritual and ethical teaching, and welcomed a partnership with them.

To meet the demand for teachers, in January 1954 James Fraser accordingly set up a Teacher Training Centre at Mbuma, 30 miles farther into the Shangani Forest than Zenka, where there was a growing population but largely heathen. Throughout Shangani, Mbuma was known by the Africans as Emakuswini among the trees and it was indeed set among lovely tall tshabella and spindly acacia trees through which the sun glinted and shimmered. In March he was joined by Katie Mary Macaulay from the Isle of Lewis, an Arts graduate of Edinburgh University. Little Thandekile Mzamo had misgivings – "Mama, does the new teacher bite?" – but Katie and James Fraser got on splendidly together. Relations with the students, some older than she, were similarly happy. She was lively and cheerful in disposition and excellent at her work – and soon won Thandekile's confidence!

Grants for boarding schools were now to be reserved for secondary schools and all Standard 4, 5 and 6 pupils would be accommodated in day-schools. Since Ingwenya Boarding School provided primary education only, it would no longer qualify for grants and would inevitably cease to exist.

The Government invited the Mission to begin secondary education with the promise of financial help for buildings and equipment. Accordingly James Tallach, who knew how to motivate the workers, set to with a swing and put up a fine school which, like the one built at Zenka, earned the encomium, "one of the finest buildings put up by Government money". With a wide entrance it was bright and airy. Above the entrance, graced by two pillars, in bold letters appeared the name, THE JOHN TALLACH SECONDARY SCHOOL.

Its first teacher was Ishbel MacCuish, an Arts graduate of Glasgow University, whose home was on the Little Cumbrae on the River Clyde. She flew out in October 1957 and, arriving in late afternoon, was met by Norman Miller, Jean, James Tallach and Mr Stewart. The Mission car was soon on its way to Ingwenya. First impressions are always interesting. "The rainy season had just started and there was a lovely green sheen over the landscape with thorn bushes scattered

James and Catherine Tallach.

The Secondary School in the late 1960s.

Mission staff pictured on the 1st January 1958. Back row, left to right: Mrs Miller and baby, Jan Van Woerden, Ishbel MacCuish, Rev James Fraser, the author, Mrs Jessie Nicolson, Miss Jean Nicolson, Mrs and Mr Stewart, James Tallach. Front row: The Miller, Stewart and Fraser children with Christina Fraser.

here and there and goats tearing at the tiny leaves. It was so wide and flat and there was a feeling of great space." To arrive when all was beginning to flower, including the jacaranda trees just inside her garden gate was to see the Mission at its best. Rev John Tallach's old house had been newly renovated. It was cool and simple in design and, when Jane returned from leave in March, between them they managed to make it quite home-like.

Till the end of the year Jane taught in the primary school but then moved into the secondary department. Jean continued as head teacher of the primary school, now known as Ingwenya Central Primary School, and was much involved in practical matters in the running of the Boarding School. The primary school boarders would be gradually phased out as the secondary department expanded. Many of the 86 boarders were former pupils of Zenka school, where Aaron Ndebele, himself a former pupil of Ingwenya, was head teacher. The five kraal schools with 500 pupils and 15 teachers were under the jurisdiction of Norman Miller.

As head teacher, Jean supervised both the academic and industrial work in the Primary School and also taught English to Standard 4 while Jane taught a section of Standard 6 full-time. There were 550 pupils and 17 African teachers. Children started to learn English from their first day in school and, as they progressed up the school, teaching was increasingly in English. As exams were in English it was in the children's interest to become as fluent as possible.

To a friend Jean wrote, "The new English Readers seem to me very difficult. Think of our Standard 4s having extracts from The Kontiki Expedition and from Churchill's Account of his Escape from the Boers! The Standard 5 and 6 readers are not out yet but I cannot imagine what heights they will rise to!"

Her Report of May 1958 was optimistic. Work to be covered in the Primary school seemed to be increasing year by year, drawing and craft now added to an already full syllabus. For craft they were doing fibre-work "as we have the materials to hand; local grasses and aloes, a kind of palm leaf which the pupils shred into long threads and weave into floor mats and table mats. Our boys evidently feel that it is a waste of valuable 'masculine' time. We are inclined to agree.

"Although we have seen many changes in the school during the past 20 years, the greatest change has been in the manner and behaviour of the boys. In 1933 there were no boys in the classes higher than Standard 2. Their attendance was spasmodic and very often before the end of the year they had been stroked off the register for poor attendance. They rode to school on donkeys and many times had to be remonstrated with for tying the poor animals to a nearby tree or to any available piece of school furniture, so that they could scarcely breathe, far less eat. In order to have a conversation with a schoolboy outside the classroom one had literally to catch him first, for as soon as he saw the European teacher approach he prepared to run. The boys were usually clad in a shirt only or in some other makeshift garment. How great the contrast now! Smartly turned out in khaki shorts and shirts, the boys are bright, responsive and rewarding to teach. Most of the boys rattle to school on second-hand bicycles, and manage to keep them in repair!"

She felt that the girls were lagging behind. True, most of the homes near Ingwenya were neat and clean and the little children much better cared for than was once the case – yet the standard of living continued to be very low. Pupils had the first meal of the day on returning from school at 2.30 pm. Their homes had little in the way of comfort with only the bare necessities – a few pots, a few spoons, a few cups and plates. Most still slept on mats on the earthen floor; fire smouldered in the middle of the floor, no chimney, smoke a-swirl. And yet these same homes might boast several bicycles, a wireless set, even a second-hand car!

"Are the women to blame for such a lop-sided state of affairs?" wondered Jean. "We are not sure. It would be a great joy to see Christian families, rather than mechanical devices and more home comforts; to see father and mother and children sitting at table together, a blessing being asked by the head of the house, and some of that order and simple dignity which we associate with any Christian home. Yet there is much to gladden the heart when visiting a real Christian home where the melody of praise and thanksgiving is heard, and kindness and affection reign."

A new era had begun! 21 January 1958 saw the first day of the John Tallach Secondary School, consisting of one classroom, a science laboratory and an office, with more buildings in prospect. The 31 pupils that first year were all boys, most of them in their late teens, all of them endowed with at least average intelligence, tremendous zeal and a high regard for learning. They regarded it as a privilege to continue beyond Standard 6 and usually it meant a sacrifice on the part of parents. Fees were paid in money, or an animal to be used for food in the Boarding School. The two-year course prepared pupils for the Rhodesian Junior Certificate, the acquisition of which was a key to further education or to more rewarding posts in industry or in the professions.

Each morning began with drill followed by Scripture. The time-table included English, Maths, Zulu, Latin, Arithmetic, Science, History and Geography. They had decided and novel ideas about the subjects they studied: to quote one boy; "I find there is a strange language. It is called Latin and has recently been invented!" Jean taught Science, and teachers were as delighted as pupils at the success of the experiments. For the students this was a new approach to learning and the hours spent in the laboratory were the highlights of the week. The science course included physics, chemistry and biology, and Jean observed, "It is an interesting speculation with some whether a little knowledge of these subjects will help to dispel the very real fear of magic and witchcraft which still prevails among even educated Africans." The actual teaching was much the same as in a European school. The chief and happiest difference was in the pupils' attitude. African children did not yet take education for granted and their teachers found their eagerness to learn endearing.

Ingwenya was a handy staging-post between Bulawayo and Shangani so there were many comings and goings either on business or pleasure. Jan van Woerden was stationed at Mbuma and James Tallach was variously engaged wherever building was in progress – and that seemed to be everywhere. Sometimes Katie came down for a weekend if she could beg a lift on the Mission lorry and they would all congregate at the Nicolsons' white-washed cottage. In the garden was a lovely bottle-brush tree with long drooping fronds while golden-shower grew profusely over the pillars which supported the roof. On the verandah they would sit exchanging news as the sun went down in the brilliant evening sky – faint turquoise, delicate

A HEART FOR AFRICA

A group leaving Mbuma on the Monday of a late 1950s Communion.
Standing in the foreground are James Tallach, John Mpofu, Philemon Ndebele,
Samuel Sitole (of Donsa Dam) and a young man from Gwamba, recently baptised.

pink, fiery orange and red. Sometimes a huge moon like a ripe, round melon sat above the horizon just as the sun was disappearing and then it would become a little silver disc in the great bowl of stars.

It was then one became aware of the sounds of Africa, so distinctively African – chirping of crickets, loud and sharp, soft cooing of doves, the clicking of cicadas or in the rainy season the clamorous croak of huge bull frogs as they splashed in the dongas and rain-pools.

The teachers liked to keep in touch with friends in missions nearby. One of the inspectors was staying at Ingwenya while he examined the kraal schools, and he invited Jean and Ishbel to go with him to Inyati Mission, the oldest mission in Southern Rhodesia. It would soon be celebrating its centenary and they were most interested to meet Robert Moffat's great-grandson there that day. There, too, were many former Ingwenya pupils, some pursuing further study and one – "a very nice good girl," said Jean – married to an African minister with the London Missionary Society.

Going into Bulawayo to meet arrivals was always something of an occasion as indeed were the corresponding farewells, though inevitably tinged with a certain sadness. So it was in June 1958 when Norman Miller and his family left for the last time. He had done a splendid job in pulling the Mission at Ingwenya together after the defection of Mr Radasi.

When Mr Stewart retired from the inspectorate and was returning to Scotland, the Ingwenya staff had a dinner and presentation for him. Mr and Mrs Stewart and their family had been good friends to the Mission and Jean maintained a lifelong friendship with them. In a farewell speech to the teachers he cautioned them against being so obsessed with exam results that they forgot that the least able were as deserving of as much attention as the most talented.

In August 1958 a refresher course was held at Ingwenya attended by 80 teachers from all denominations in the area. James Fraser gave the opening address on the teaching of Scripture under the title, "The Gospel of our Lord Jesus Christ", in which he considered the gospel as a message from God, an experience and a way of life. Such occasions meant hard work but the benefit, both professional and spiritual, not to mention the making and cementing of friendships was, all were agreed, worth every panic-stricken moment of preparation.

At the end of that year James Fraser was due to go home on a much-needed leave. He had been suffering ill health off and on during the past five years and his work-load was crushing. In the style of the early missionaries he did not spare himself; he was preacher, teacher, tutor, dentist and administrator of 23 schools with 3000 pupils and over 80 teachers. In difficult circumstances he had shown exemplary forbearance and understanding. His wife, Chris, ran a busy clinic. The strain had told on the health of both and they were looking forward to a rest and a refreshing reunion with their families in Scotland. It was arranged that Teacher Training should be moved to Ingwenya for the year he would be on leave, a heavy responsibility for Katie, but she was equal to the task.

Their passage was booked for early January. In December Mr Fraser took ill. It began with a severe headache and other symptoms. James Tallach, in most difficult circumstances, managed to bring him down to hospital in Bulawayo by car – the rainy season made roads all but impassable. He was diagnosed with a viral infection. His doctors used their best skill and he responded somewhat to treatment but it was only a temporary respite. Norman Miller, at home in London, spared no effort in enlisting help but all available drugs proved ineffectual. His resigned and uncomplaining spirit impressed doctors and nurses.

Jan van Woerden was a regular visitor and Mr Fraser appreciated their times of prayer together. Jan remembered his ongoing practical interest in all Mission affairs; "He continued to serve the cause of Christ on his sickbed until he had no more strength to speak. After having talked on business matters for some

The Rev. James Fraser,
1913-1959.
"Thandabantu" – "The man who loved the people."

time with effort, forcing his weary brain to concentrate, he would suddenly whisper with a sigh, 'It is quiet now; let us have a few words of prayer before we are disturbed.'" Drugs from America were sent for and were at first effective but by that time it was too late. On Saturday, 28 March 1959 he died, aged 45.

Thandabantu, the man who loved the people, was buried the following Monday in the small graveyard at Ingwenya beside his infant son, among the people he loved. Mrs Fraser returned to Scotland with little Elizabeth, Isobel and baby Cameron later that year. Her health was broken and she died two years later.

The Ingwenya staff wrote, "Words cannot express our deep sense of loss at the passing of our dear friend and colleague, the Rev James Fraser. So wise and gracious, so rich in human sympathy, he gave his life to the service of the Master."

Jean put the thoughts of many succinctly: "His gain – our loss; but also, I feel, a warning to us not again to allow a young, enthusiastic missionary to be so overworked."

● CHAPTER **13** ●

Our Loss Their Gain

AFTER the months of anxiety the Mission staff were greatly encouraged by the arrival of Rev Alfred MacDonald in August. It was good to have a regular ministry again. His first sermon was on the text, "Other men laboured and ye are entered into their labours." He had taught for some years in secondary schools in Scotland so, as well as carrying out his pastoral duties, he shared in the educational side of the work.

The staff at Ingwenya were delighted to have Katie with them running the Teacher Training course. Classes of the primary school were used for teaching practice and Jean, whose experience was invaluable, often helped Katie with advice and by giving criticisms of lessons – crits in educational jargon; the student would teach while Jean or Katie observed how he went about the task. A lesson plan was submitted first of all detailing what the student was trying to accomplish and how he intended to achieve this. Later there would be a discussion with him as to how far he had succeeded, what was commendable, what needed attention – his manner of speaking, clarity of presentation, use of questions, appeal to the imagination, how he dealt with obvious misunderstandings and a host of other considerations. Students were put in full charge of a class for three weeks at a time; it was found that this training made for a self-reliant teacher.

Numbers in the boarding school were growing and supervision took ever more time and energy. Each evening some of the teachers went over to the dormitories to bid the boarders "Goodnight" and they liked that. "They were happy and full of fun, diving into bed and under blankets at our approach. It was a struggle to pull them up to the crazy Amakiwa [white] standards of order but the general atmosphere was one of good-humour with respect and affection and not much need at all for harsh discipline. I think we saw the best of them in the early years when they believed that the Europeans were there for their sakes. It was a happy and carefree time.

"Jean knew the African psyche well and could throw off teasing remarks to the pupils in Ndebele. This they loved. She liked young people and got on well with them. The pupils were well-mannered. These were the early days. Times changed and manners too as political awareness grew.

"The sheer pressure of work could be wearing – teaching, preparation, corrections, supervision of study times, lighting the tilley lamps for use in the evenings – never enough mantles, flying ants attracted to the light swirling to their death and leaving a heap of wings and a smell of singeing."

Friday evenings were free and then it was dressing in one's best and enjoying some simple fun and games as a change from studies. Saturday mornings were divided between studies and manual work when flower beds were tended, paths cleared, a netball pitch laid out and classrooms swept while a teacher encouraged or hustled as necessary. Afternoons were spent on the playing field, and the evenings devoted to preparation for the Sabbath.

In the debating club the teenage makers and breakers of public opinion held forth on subjects of topical interest – for example, "Women should not have the same education as men". Africans are ready speakers and the splendid displays of oratory surprised and impressed their teachers. And sometimes amused them.

A topic that turned up over and over again was the question of lobola. A man wishing to marry must first of all ask her father for the girl's hand. The two men would then come to an agreement as to how much lobola, either in money or cattle, the prospective groom should pay the bride's father. Lobola might be spread over many years but, as long as it was not fully paid, the woman's father had right over any children of the marriage. In fact sometimes a child or two might be handed over in lieu of unpaid lobola, the parents thus losing all authority over them.

A girl might be promised in marriage while still a child and the father forthwith received his cattle. When the time came for her to marry, unless her father could repay the lobola – and drought or dire necessity might have impoverished him in the interim – she would be forced to go through with the marriage regardless of her own feelings in the matter.

Polygamy was a difficult question. The best solution as far as the Church was concerned, but one which still left problems, seemed to be that those who wished to profess Christianity must agree to keep the first wife and send the others back to their family homes. The practice of polygamy was fraught with the possibility of much mischief. Attending John Tallach school were Sitabile and her very clever, younger brother. He had a sad, haunted look about him and when their family history was known it was no surprise that they did not want to go home, ever. First their mother, the prettiest and youngest of a number of wives, was poisoned by the others, then their father died. To such children school was a refuge.

Sometimes the women asserted themselves. "The other day the several wives of a nuisance of a man who used to treat them just like slaves, tied him to a tree and gave him a sound beating! They must have been really driven to it as the wives are so subservient and normally don't think of rebelling."

A widow had few rights. Her husband's brother had the right to her property, including her children, and even the widow herself though this she was free to refuse. She was thus left in a very vulnerable situation.

Usually when a son married he brought his wife to his father's kraal – and he might well end up with several wives. The other sons would do likewise so that there would eventually be quite a little community of brothers and sisters and half-brothers and cousins.

This is reflected in their vocabulary. Ubaba can refer to a child's father, his father's brothers, and the husbands of his mother's sisters; likewise umama can refer to his mother, his mother's sisters and the wives of his mother's brothers. Brothers, step-brothers, half-brothers, first cousins are all referred to as brothers – or sisters as may be. So he may have umpteen brothers and sisters. And that's not counting the possible permutations of polygamy!

It was quite common for children to be transferred from one home to another; in fact, to find a family all living under one roof was rare. Jean observed, "This communal attitude runs as a pattern through life and manifests itself in small ways in the Mission where one child speaks of another as sister Martha or brother Benjamin, or when a new coat, discriminatingly given to a delicate child, is eaten in, slept in, and worn threadbare by all the other members of her house apparently without protest from her."

On Saturday afternoons, as it became cooler, Jean and one or two of the others would sometimes take a walk around the Mission, visiting the dormitories and simply "being seen". John Mpofu, over 80 but still smart and alert, lived in a small thatched hut in the middle of the Mission compound and they often stopped as they passed near and heard him on his knees in prayer.

As a young man he had been one of Lobengula's bodyguards and was subsequently employed as a gardener by the Wesleyan minister in Bulawayo. He had never been to school and could not read. It was the custom among missionaries that their employees must attend their church. One day the minister passed through the garden and held up the Bible he was carrying; "This is the Word of God and God is speaking to you in this Book, John." John glanced up and resumed his work.

A few days later the minister again spoke to him, "This Book is speaking to you, John, telling you that you are a sinner and that you need a Saviour." John did not seem to understand.

The next time the minister appeared it was John who spoke. "I want that Book you have in your hand."

"But you can't read and I have only seven copies. I must give them to people who can read."

"I want it! You say the Book is speaking to me so I want it." His persistence paid off and at home he persisted in prayer that God would teach him to read.

In the absence of a minister he frequently took services at Ingwenya and read Scripture so beautifully that, as Jean said, "it was as good as any sermon." His sermons were short but animated and to the point. Jean remembered some of his sayings and prayers. "Children of the Matabele, children of the Matabele, who ever heard of a king dying for his people? It is the people who die for their king, but King Jesus died for His people – a great and solemn thought which drives away sleep when it comes to one at night." He often quoted in prayer, "If ye seek Me, let these go their way." Ingwenya he called Jerusalem wetu, our Jerusalem.

His son Alexander had been head teacher at Nkai, where his wife also taught, but for the last 12 years he had been engaged in full-time missionary work.

Jean often spoke of the early days of the Mission when she had the privilege, and she counted it a great one, of knowing men such as Philemon Ndebele, Joseph Nombembe, John Ncube, Isaiah Nyati and Robert Komence. She honoured these men for their godly lives and could quote some expressions and petitions from their prayers. She recognised true piety and esteemed it in everyone but said there was something special about these early converts.

With all the wealth of interest that Rhodesia and South Africa had to offer, holidays were thoroughly enjoyed if only for the change of scene.

Mrs Nicolson and Jean often stayed in mission rest-homes where they met and made friends of missionaries from a variety of backgrounds. The hotels and lodges offered a piquant contrast to their normal life and they enjoyed the touch of luxury. It was a novelty to be awakened by the cheeky vervet monkeys chattering on the verandah outside or the unexpectedly raucous call of the neat and spruce little weaver birds. This attractive native of Rhodesia with bright yellow plumage and black head builds its nest to hang from the very tip of a branch of a tree in an attempt to escape the attentions of snakes and other predators.

The Victoria Falls were even more awe-inspiring than they had imagined. Well might Livingstone exclaim, "A sight for angels to gaze on!" A mile wide, the waters can be heard several miles away thundering 400 feet down to a narrow gorge.

The Falls are on the edge of the Hwange Game Park and to view animals in the wild was a totally different experience from a visit to a zoo. It was therapeutic to have dinner round an outdoor fire at sundown, that dulcet time of day when all seems right with the world, to watch the animals emerge from the forest and come down in leisurely but purposeful procession to the pools – the astonishing giraffe, legs splayed as it reaches down to drink, the graceful impala, masterful kudu and the sturdy zebra, all with their entourage of young, playing, luxuriating, squirting, but always wary.

A visit to the Kruger National Park afforded an unforgettable experience of another kind. As they drove along within the speed limit there was a sudden crash of timber and an elephant emerged from the tangle of tree and frond and planted itself on the track just ahead of them, trunk swaying. They knew better than to disturb him by movement or sound and waited until he plodded off. On looking back they saw that the huge creature was making after them, ears flapping. Driving as fast as they dared they just managed to outdistance it. Not long after this they heard of a carload of tourists

African elephant.

who came upon an elephant in the middle of the track and imperiously hooted at it. Excited, or angered, it simply lifted its foot and brought it down on the car, crushing it and its occupants.

Lake Kariba, the second-largest man-made lake in the world was now the main source of electricity for Zimbabwe and Zambia and they felt it deserved a visit so one school holiday a group took a trip to see the recently-constructed dam. The lake had swallowed up a forest from where 40,000 Tonga were moved, some to Binga where in the future the Free Presbyterian Church would start a work.

Above: ruins at Great Zimbabwe.
Below: visit to Bembesi Dam.

Great Zimbabwe, meaning "great stone house", had been the chiefs' court and a centre of religious ritual. These prehistoric ruins

A HEART FOR AFRICA

near Masvingo had massive walls 40 feet high in places and up to 12 feet thick. Within the Great Enclosure stood high conical look-out towers. Granite blocks, brick-shaped and about twice the size of bricks, fit so closely together – without mortar – that a knife blade cannot be slipped between them.

Nearer home they enjoyed occasional trips into town. Bulawayo was a spacious colonial city with an air of unhurried ease. Cecil Rhodes had stipulated that the roads must be wide enough for a span of eight oxen to turn around and so the wide avenues, bordered by jacaranda trees, were laid out on this plan. The parks were graced by tropical plants and shrubs and giant indigenous trees. By the park the vendors of crochet, embroidery, wood carvings and beadwork hopefully coaxed passing tourists to buy. A visit to Haddon and Sly, the up-market department store on Fife Street, was mandatory. Upstairs was the place where ladies met to sip tea and gossip. There might be friends to visit. Mr and Mrs Stevenson, whom they had met on one of their holidays, generously entertained the Mission folk and maintained a friendship with the Nicolsons over many years. Then it was home with groceries and small treats. The car often broke down on the way; the dry river beds and half-hidden tree-stumps tested car and driver.

These outings were especially appreciated since the staff were often weeks on end without leaving the Mission. In term Saturday afternoons were usually spent preparing work, supervising the boarders, visiting the Line and such necessary activities.

Jean was able to devote all the necessary time to her work because Mrs Nicolson took full responsibility in the home. She was a superb and interested cook. There was one fruit that she wondered about; she asked the local women about it and discovered that they never used it. She experimented and found that it could be made into quite a palatable jam.

Her many talents and interests, mostly of the practical kind, included dress-making, crafts, gardening. "She never flags unless she has been overdoing it and her heart objects," commented one of the teachers. "Just over a year ago she had a serious heart attack. In fact she was not expected to live. Today she was putting in some rose-cuttings and so enthusiastic about it. Her hobby is hens, and yesterday she brought home 25 new chicks from town."

In the dispensary her advice was frequently sought, and her battle with the snake fraternity was as unrelenting as it had ever been. Anti-snake-bite serum was now available but not often required, though from time to time there were incidents. A preacher was returning home after taking a service one Sabbath. He had strapped his Zulu Bible behind him on the carrier of his bicycle before hopping on. Inadvertently he ran over a snake which started to pursue him. Pedalling for his life he made off at top speed and to his horror heard a loud crack. Arrived home he found the mark of the fangs on his Bible.

One of the teachers, newly awake one morning, became aware of a slight movement and watched, numb, as a snake slowly made its way along the roof beam that ran above her bed. As it drew nearer she scarcely dared breathe but concentrated on keeping as still as stone. Nearer it came and nearer till it was overhead and slithered under the open eave and out. She jumped up, threw on a coat and ran for James Tallach. "Come quick! There's a snake!" He grabbed his gun and soon despatched it.

James was overseeing the building of a new church at Ingwenya. The old corrugated-iron one built away back in Mr Radasi's day was now too small, and very hot in summer. He took a real pride in the work he did and the new red-brick church, the third on that site, was bright and well-ventilated. James was up late and early painting and varnishing, for the Governor of Rhodesia was about to pay a visit and there was feverish activity to ensure that the Mission did itself credit.

After the formal reception and an informal tea-party with the local teachers His Excellency visited several classrooms and listened in to some lessons before looking in at the boys' dormitory which was, averred Jean, "for the only time before and since, in perfect order. Two rows of 30 beds arrayed in covers of rainbow coloured print, a gift from our Canadian friends, against a background of whitewashed walls and large airy windows made a charming picture. The school dining-room looked scarcely less attractive with its long white tables and green and white walls."

At the end of 1959 Teacher Training had been closed down. Katie was due leave and Jane was retiring after 14 years of fruitful work. On New Year's Day they were to sail from Cape Town and a group

OUR LOSS THEIR GAIN

of friends saw them off at Bulawayo station. Katie recalled, "Mrs Nicolson, although she had not been feeling very fit, had bravely made the effort to come to the station but failed in her attempt to walk the length of the platform."

For some time it had been apparent to those around her that her health was failing. However, when she felt a little better she would be up and about, busying herself with whatever her energy would allow – perhaps embroidery or attending to her hens or her collection of African violets in delicate shades of pink, mauve, purple, with the most beautiful leaves – and she still took a lively interest in Mission affairs. In July 1960 she was admitted to hospital in Bulawayo for an emergency operation for appendicitis and made a good recovery. But her strength had gone.

It was a great sorrow to African and European alike to see her become frail and on Sabbath, 5 March 1961, she died. Rev Alfred MacDonald, whose visits during her illness she greatly valued, wrote, "The remains of Mrs Nicolson were laid in the small graveyard here at Ingwenya to await the glorious resurrection. Thus she came to her end here 'like as a shock of corn cometh in in his season.' The loss to the Mission is great. Her interest was both intelligent and spiritual. To her daughter, who tirelessly attended to her while busy with the many other duties on the Mission, we extend sympathy." A stone was erected in her memory and that of Mackinlay. Inscribed on it are words of Psalm 50, "Call upon Me in the day of trouble: I will deliver thee."

The news of her death was heard with profound sorrow throughout the Church. Mother and daughter had become something of an institution so that many who had never met her felt the impact of her going. The *Free Presbyterian Magazine* of April 1961 carried a short tribute; "Mrs Nicolson manifested much love to the Lord and His Cause in the Mission in her great and constant devotion to every duty laid to her hand. The grace of the Lord and her various and conspicuous gifts made her a Mother in Israel to Europeans and Africans alike. We extend our deepest sympathy to Miss Nicolson and to all sorrowing friends in Southern Rhodesia. In concluding this note, we would remind readers that an old, godly elder, John Mpofu, recently died on the Mission. The late Mrs Nicolson and John were great friends, and so white and black who fear the Lord go 'to be with Christ which is far better' when death removes them from the world."

Jean wrote, "On 5th March my dear Mother passed away, we believe to her eternal rest. I should like to acknowledge the goodness of the Most High in leaving her with me so long. She often used to quote with regard to our congregation here, 'And give Him no rest until He establish and till He make Jerusalem a praise in the earth.'"

Starting off in a modest little house with no ceiling they had set an example of gracious living that was unrivalled on the Mission even when amenities were greatly improved.

Before going on furlough in August Jean was pleased to learn that Marion Graham, a niece of Mrs Tallach, was coming to help in the Secondary department. Flying out with her in October was Catherine Tallach, who would be most welcome at Mbuma Hospital. Etta MacLennan arrived just before the beginning of the new session in January. Ello MacKenzie and Lilian Fraser joined the teaching staff at that time also.

Mbuma Mission Hospital.

● Chapter 14 ●

Changes

I T was May 1963. Rev Petros Mzamo and Mr Alexander Mpofu were in Scotland and were invited to address the annual Synod of their Church in Inverness. Mr Mzamo, had for the past six years been minister of Mbuma church. Now he was elected Moderator, the first African to hold such a position in a Scottish church. He made a forceful plea that the missionaries should all learn Ndebele: "The people love to hear it!" The whole psalter in Ndebele metre had just been published and the people were overjoyed. Previously only some psalms had been in Ndebele metre and the Zulu version of the psalter had been used in church, but now they could sing all the psalms in their own tongue.

In August, after a visit to Canada, Jean was back at Ingwenya. In daylight the most noticeable feature was the number of new buildings. But the great surprise came at night – the Mission was a blaze of light! Back in 1949 she and Mr McPherson had written to the Foreign Missions Committee with detailed costings for connecting the Mission to the electricity grid which ran near Ingwenya, but for some reason it was not until 1960 that electricity was installed. "It was a great day when the tilley lamps became history," wrote someone who was there at the time, "and we began to enjoy . . . electricity for light, fridges and other household amenities. It seemed like luxury but we soon got used to it".

A primary class at Ingwenya.

Jean was soon immersed in her role as Head of the large Primary School. Numbers were now hovering around the 500 mark. Among the 17 teachers were four who in the previous year had been boarders in the secondary school. Approximately half the staff were trained so she was virtually engaged in training the others. With a competent and sympathetic guide this proved quite an effective method but it was time-consuming, and of course the pupils suffered while the fledgling teacher was finding her way. Jean had an excellent relationship with them and they tried to live up to her exacting standards. With almost half the staff untrained, the standard in attainment had inevitably gone down and to reverse that trend would require a mammoth effort and much skill. She also had oversight of 11 teachers in four out-schools – Cameron, Libeni, Maqaqeni and Gobola.

The dispensary became the responsibility of whomsoever had the nerve to act as nurse, and in practice probably all the teachers had their turn with more or less success. And as Marion discovered, "the psychological effect of a good big bandage, even when made out of an old sheet, is very great!"

More teachers were coming out from Scotland and as staff increased, all agreed that the good relations and smooth running of the Mission were largely due to Jean. She was a dedicated teacher with high standards in her professional as in her personal life and never lost sight of the primary aim of the Mission: to bring the gospel to those she worked among, and to instil Christian principles in teachers and pupils.

Inspectors in Bulawayo thought so much of the Ingwenya set-up that the school was considered a model of its kind. One inspector confessed that they kept their inspection of Ingwenya as a treat with which to finish their rota. They were very pleasant and would join in evening worship, singing the psalms and kneeling for prayer. Mr Bird expressed himself as being specially impressed by the beauty of the psalm-singing. They also enjoyed the delights of Mrs Nicolson's table!

The school day began at 7 am but in Africa it was easy to rise at 6 am when the air was alive with birdsong and the sun was dispelling the darkness of the veldt. First came 15 minutes of drill. The children had a fine feeling for rhythm which was evident in their hand-clapping games and other exercises. Most were smart in school uniform – boys in khaki shirts and shorts, girls in green tunics with white blouses.

Many of the primary classes were held out of doors under a tree or on the wide grassy rectangle between the two long red-brick school buildings facing each other. In the centre of this rectangle was a cement map of the world so it was a natural spot on which to conduct a history or geography lesson. When the British Isles were pointed out there were invariably gasps of amazement, "Ah! Ah! So small, so tiny!"

•

The 58 secondary pupils ranged in age from 14 to 25 years so some of them were young adults. The main criterion for admittance to the secondary school was in general that they should have the relevant qualifications and local children would normally have priority. When applicants greatly outnumbered places available an examination was set to help the head teacher make the final decision. The two-year Junior Certificate course gave access to teacher training, nursing, or apprenticeship into one of the trades. Alternatively one could proceed to other centres of learning to do the Cambridge Certificate, which involved a further two years of study. All 63 secondary pupils and 81 from the upper classes of the primary school were housed in two dormitory blocks equipped with sanitation and electric light.

In the school there was a social mix to gladden the heart of the most committed egalitarian. The pupils' background might be heathen, nominally Christian or one of the variety of sects. Some were from truly Christian homes. Fathers were rich or poor, educated or uneducated. Pupils included the sons of chiefs. Sekai Hove, daughter of a Member of the Federal Parliament, wrote to thank her teacher for the spiritual teaching she had received.

Zororai Mazwabo, a Shona, arrived as a rather reluctant student. At the end of his primary education at a mission about 50 miles from Ingwenya he was anxious to find a place in a secondary school. He knew of the John Tallach School but had no wish to go there. He had no interest in the gospel and had heard that there he would be "tortured – made to read the Bible all day," as he later confessed. "I must say I was very much afraid of that." Anyway, he told himself, no need to fear; he would find a place in a Government school. But the Government school had no place for him; too old, they said – although another applicant, older than he, was accepted! "Don't worry," his headmaster said, "I've managed to get a place for you at Ingwenya."

"Oh no, I'm not going there!"

"Very well, I'll get you a place elsewhere." But soon after that the teacher died, suddenly. Zororai knew he had no hope of finding a place on his own so he contacted Ingwenya to see if the offer was still open. It was and "very soon I found out that I was not tortured."

Not only did he find Ingwenya bearable but he was soon revising his views at a more fundamental level. One day after some trouble among the boys Mr MacDonald said to Zororai that the Shona pupils had been a cause of dissension in the school and on the Mission. Zororai answered politely, "Perhaps some of the Shona pupils are more interested in the gospel you preach than the Matabele are." After training as a teacher Zororai taught for some years in a school at some distance from Ingwenya. The gospel truths he had heard at Ingwenya bore fruit and the staff were encouraged to hear news of his conversion. He was accepted as a student for the ministry and later became a missionary to the Shona people; he held his first service under a tree with a congregation of four women and a few children.

Though things were generally quiet at Ingwenya there was continuing unrest throughout the country. African leaders were demanding black majority rule and no longer could one command respect solely on account of the colour of one's skin. There was a tendency to denounce Christianity as the white man's way of taming Africans in order to take their land. Joshua Nkomo, leader of the Africa National Congress, urged his followers to return to ancestor worship and there was a resurgence of African customs such as umbuyiso and uku-thethela.

There were sporadic flare-ups at Zenka and Mbuma, also rioting in Bulawayo, and then all would be quiet for a time. The Post Office in Bulawayo was damaged by a bomb put through a letter box. During one riot some of the Ingwenya pupils were caught unawares in the African Location. As people retreated indoors they found themselves suddenly vulnerable. Grabbing sticks they waved them aloft and joined in the fracas yelling, "Kwacha, kwacha! Freedom, freedom!" So they made their getaway and reached the Mission unscathed.

One night at Zenka the alarm was raised when two classrooms were found ablaze. Men came running from the nearby kraals and all battled to contain the conflagration but the buildings were completely gutted. One of the teachers grabbed her camera and managed to get some spectacular snapshots. The hooligan element was suspected and the perpetrators were quickly caught.

Some missions in Shangani were stoned but neither Zenka nor Mbuma were affected. When Jan and Margaret van Woerden went on leave in April, Catherine Tallach was left in sole charge of the hospital. As she would be the only white person in Mbuma the District Commissioner was most concerned. "You must not leave her alone. The situation is so volatile and there is no possibility of help getting there quickly." "Oh, there's no need to worry!" he was told. "The Africans love her – she's just like one of themselves. She is the safest person in Shangani!"

Group photo taken in 1965. Left to right: Catherine Tallach, Reta Carmichael, Margaret van Woerden with Hugo, Lilian Fraser, Mary MacInnes, Ishbel MacCuish and Jean.

In Southern Rhodesia apartheid had never existed on the same scale as in South Africa, but naturally it was a source of trouble and justifiable complaint. One of the Mbuma missionaries was in a store with an African minister – a dignified, well-educated man older than himself. To his chagrin he was told by the store-keeper, "Tell your boy to go to the other counter!"

Many Europeans were well-disposed to their employees and treated them with respect but a few instances of rudeness were enough to incite resentment – and there were more than a few. The burning issue was that, as an African, one was not due equal respect with the European; if respect came his way it was regarded as a courtesy rather than as a right. One perceptive African noticed that some of the friction was due to simple misunderstanding: "Our way of thinking is different from your way of thinking. An African may speak to a European with all respect and courtesy but it may appear to the European that the African is cheeky. That is because of his way of thinking."

In 1965, after the Unilateral Declaration of Independence under Premier Ian Smith, the British Government imposed sanctions against Rhodesia. One immediate consequence was that no money might be sent from the United Kingdom to the Mission. The matter was brought up in Parliament. Hansard records a speech in which it was pointed out to the Chancellor of the Exchequer that the contributions sent out to the Mission were for salaries to "missionaries there who are teaching African children. Is he aware that these salaries are already far less than the salaries which these people would receive in this country and that to offer them three-quarters of these salaries when they are away from home . . . is quite unreasonable?" The permissible amount was raised but funds were still totally inadequate.

However, there had been growing interest in the Mission among supporters in Holland and in 1964 Mbuma Zending was formed for the support, initially, of the hospital at Mbuma but soon for the whole work of the Mission. There were no restrictions, of course, on Holland sending money to Rhodesia and in these difficult circumstances the timely help from the new Society was invaluable – and continued year after year.

The political unrest did not appreciably affect the school at Ingwenya except that there was an added interest in African history! As for the people, they continued to welcome the missionaries into their homes as warmly as ever.

What the people around Ingwenya and in Shangani felt even more than sanctions was the severe famine which affected Matabeleland, and to some extent the whole of southern Africa, for almost three years. The Ntabazinduna area was particularly hard hit. Between March 1965 and the end of the following January there were only two showers. Some missions were forced to close for lack of water and for two years in succession there were no crops. Jean wrote, "The people ploughed and planted but no mealie plants appeared or, if they did, it was to shrivel up and die. The cattle searched in vain for even a few blades of grass. The wells began to

Opposite: The cover of the programme of lectures and talks given at the Mbuma Zending Day held at Utrecht on 18 July 1964. Rev. Donald MacLean of Glasgow spoke from Malachi 3:17: "And they shall be mine, saith the Lord of hosts, in that day when I make up my jewels."

Mbuma - zending

Toespraken en referaten

**VAN DE OP 18 JULI 1964 TE UTRECHT
GEHOUDEN ZENDINGSDAG**

40e jaargang no. 11
juli 2008

Want het sal geschieden ten
selven dage, dat de heidenen
naar den Wortel Isai,
Die staan sal tot een
banier der volkeren, sullen
vragen, ende Zijne ruste
sal heerlijk zijn.

Jesaja 11:10

Mbuma

MAANDBLAD VAN DE NEDERLANDSE STICHTING MBUMA-ZENDING

A HEART FOR AFRICA

dry up and in December the Mission well at Ingwenya had as little as three feet of water." Thousands of cattle were lost. Wildlife died and starving animals were killed by desperate people. A woman who walked ten miles to Zenka in search of food told her friend there that she had put her crying children to bed, hoping they would sleep while she was looking for help.

The people did as best they could, scraping around for roots and berries. One woman was delighted to find a wild plant with green berries which she heard were safe to eat if boiled for a whole day and night and then left for another day before venturing to eat. She tried it and lived to recommend the recipe!

Drought with consequent famine was a recurring aspect of life with which the people had to contend. Mr Mzamo spoke of how the sight of emaciated faces weighed down the spirits. "It is a painful experience to try to preach to a hungry congregation. It is the same experience with the nurses at the hospital and the teachers at the school. Treating hungry patients, teaching starving pupils." To witness children fainting for lack of food, mothers collapsing with hunger was heart-wrenching. When settled in New Canaan Rev Z Mazvabo felt the same overwhelming compassion. "Those who have not experienced famine find it difficult to imagine what straits famine brings people to. . . . It overshadows everything. . . . When services start and I see them fall asleep, their lips looking whitish and dry, I am sharply reminded that they have nothing to eat . . . . Starvation and disease seem to go hand in hand."

He wrote of the tension in a home where the mother does not know where the next meal is coming from: "Perhaps for people in distant and well-watered lands it might not be easy to understand how cruel a famine can be. It just upsets every avenue of life and brings misunderstanding in an otherwise peaceful home. Father begins to think that mother is wasteful, while mother and children think that father is not doing enough to provide for the family. Young boys and girls have to move away from home early in search of employment – so that not only is their social life affected but also their religious life."

Unemployment and stress-related illness add to the distress. And among the more ignorant there is the anxiety as to what is making the spirits so angry. Are there human bones lying around unburied somewhere? What do these stones lying on top of one another mean? Is that an omen? When the rains come the few animals left are often too weak to plough and the people, weak and hungry though they be, must dig the ground themselves. In desperate circumstances the children may have to be yoked to the plough but the hope of harvest gives courage.

The Government did what it could to help but the need was vast, and many went for days with nothing to eat. The Mission provided maize for the poor near Ingwenya and a specially nutritious soup for the young children. Sabbath School children from Scotland had been sending money to buy food but after UDI this source of help was cut off. Donations from Canada and elsewhere enabled the missionaries to meet some of the most pressing need in Ntabazinduna and the Fingo Locations.

Jean was at last able to report: "Late in January, and almost at the end of the rainy season, the drought ended. Heavy rains fell and in a few weeks' time the whole countryside was green once more, rivers ran, the wells filled and the dams overflowed."

But crops do not grow overnight. People constantly came to the back door of the mission houses and there was no need to ask if they were hungry; then off they would go happy, small bag balanced on head. Most of them would reap no maize at all that year in the entire area and that meant that for a whole year to come they would be on the edge of starvation. The teachers were glad to help. "So far we have been able to supply all who come to us but it is very tiring hauling out bags many times a day – however it's good to be able to do it and a pleasure really," was their attitude.

It was at the back door that news of the local doings was relayed. It was there that they heard of a former pupil, a girl, who was drowned after being attacked by a crocodile. Patson Ncube, a boy of 15 who left Ingwenya school in December 1964 was swept away when crossing a causeway near his home and was similarly attacked. Such events cast a gloom over the mission community and especially their class-mates.

And sometimes an unexpected treat came their way as recounted in one letter: "Sidingani's parcel arrived today. What a lovely surprise he will get. Only I won't be here to see his reaction. I am glad you worded the birthday card as you did so that the others will accept the reason for Sidingani's 'good fortune'. Incidentally Sidingani means 'what are we looking for?' It's a lovely parcel. The jersey will fit him and I think I shall ask his teacher to share the sweets with the rest of the class. Perhaps Sidingani will think of that himself. A thousand thanks! His teacher will show him how to play Chinese Chequers and they can all have a turn at it. He is a very nice boy, the kind you like to see getting a treat. Ma Tshuma was with me all day. She is feeling ill these days and hasn't a scrap of food apart from what we give her." This old church member was one of those who benefited from the many parcels of clothing received. She later went up to Mbuma and refused to return till harvest time when she intended to haul back a stock of food for the winter!

"Last Saturday afternoon there was a spectacular thunderstorm and when it passed Jean decided we should take mealie-meal to a few needy people using the old stuttery truck. On the way back we had a puncture and no tools. A car came along to help but they had no proper tools and had to go careering off to find some. A crowd gathered round and a woman brought out a brazier with bright burning sticks – lovely and warm; it was a bitter cold evening with piercing wind. We had a lovely time round the brazier while the others worked. The whole operation took about two hours." A striking feature of the country was how ready people were to help.

"We are selling the rickety grey truck soon and buying another. It has acquired such a personality with its idiosyncrasies that we feel quite a pang to realise that we shall soon be back to orthodoxy. The other day when we were returning from Bembesi both doors kept flying open, so eventually we just let the driver's door swing to and fro on its hinges. The engine was spluttering and grunting, the gears were screeching. The amazing thing is that it always gets you where you want to go."

In the Line they encountered sore need. On one of these outings they were accompanied by a visitor from Scotland who wrote, "On

Saturday we were at Jean's for dinner and then went to the Line to visit a sick boy. Oh, they're miserable-looking dwellings, so small, with a fire on the floor in the middle and the boy huddled under a bundle of rags by the fire. In fact I didn't know he was there and might have trodden on him. The people were so friendly and gave me a basket of eggs." The poor lad was very ill. One eye protruded as if, to the untutored mind of the visitors, there was a tumour behind it. Yet there was no sign of self-pity or disgruntlement. His gracious appreciation of a mere visit lent him a dignity that cancelled out the pitifulness of his situation.

Subsequent letters told an all-too-familiar story of reluctance to seek medical attention till too late: "Thomas is getting worse and pills don't help now. His parents won't hear of his going to hospital and the last word lies with them. He is so nice and polite – a really attractive boy despite his appearance. You get very attached to these poor people – especially when they depend on you for food as well as for everything else." Later, "Thomas was asking for you one day. I was surprised that he remembered you. He is getting worse." And finally success, so far, "Jean and I hope to go to town tomorrow to take Thomas to the specialist at Mpilo [Hospital]. His father has at last consented. He's now very, very ill and it's a last resort from the parents' point of view. We hope at least they can alleviate his pain . . . . ." Treatment helped temporarily and there was hope that shortly before he died Thomas became a Christian.

Aaron Ndebele, head teacher at Zenka was accepted for the ministry and, after studying with Rev Alfred MacDonald, set off to do his final studies in Scotland. One of those seeing him off on the plane wrote, "He was like a happy schoolboy waving a cheerful goodbye just before he popped inside. He has such a warm, pleasing personality. He will be absolutely delighted to have done with the colour bar for six months. He gets so upset at times over the treatment; it is so demeaning. Aaron is, of course, in favour of Independence with an African Prime Minister at the head of government in a multi-racial society."

When he returned, the Europeans were eager to hear his news and frank views of their homeland. The families from Zenka and Mbuma met together on such occasions if possible. As the staff expanded and young families were growing up, Jean and the others took a lively interest in the children. One was pronounced "not bonnie in the conventional sense but with a good strong face full of character".

"A Deborah," agreed Jean. At age four months!

The situation in the church at Ingwenya was much more settled than for the past several years and Rev Alfred MacDonald had accepted a call to Gairloch in Scotland. His ministry had been much appreciated by many who felt a real sense of loss at his going. On 26 June 1966 the church was packed to capacity when Rev A Ndebele was ordained and inducted to the pastoral charge of Ingwenya. Two lorry loads of women arrived from Shangani singing psalms in Ndebele, the waves of sound announcing their approach from some distance. Greetings were exchanged and the adults took their places. Then in marched the secondary pupils smart in black school blazers with a distinctive badge designed by Marion. The badge had a Bible and lamp against the St Andrew's cross and the words, "Thy Word is a lamp". As many of the younger children as could manage squashed onto benches at the front and the rest squatted on the floor, using up every available inch. Rev P Mzamo

Rev A Ndebele at the Centenary Commemoration Meeting of the Free Presbyterian Church of Scotland, held in the Church of Scotland Assembly Hall, Edinburgh, on Tuesday, 25th May 1993, at which Mr Ndebele gave a lecture on aspects of the Zimbabwean Mission.
On his left is the Rev J R Tallach who gave many years of service as a doctor on the Mission.

preached from the words, "Let a man so count of us, as of the ministers of Christ, and as stewards of the mysteries of God."

After the service there was a plentiful picnic under the trees, prepared by the Mission staff. Then it was time to leave with cries of "Hambane guhle! Goodbye!" as the women clambered onto the backs of their lorries with much heaving and shoving and the men on to theirs, all singing.

Mr Ndebele was a lively preacher and gradually many of those who had gone off with Mr Radasi returned. There was an upsurge of interest generally. A voluntary Bible Study Group for teachers was held every alternate Friday evening, at which Paul's Epistle to the Romans was studied. The question asked most frequently was, "How can a person know whether he is truly converted?" Discussion groups, called "Timothy's" were formed among the boarders and were held on Saturdays. In the Sabbath school there were on average 270 children each week.

There was often a genuine conflict in the minds of these young people between what they learned in school and what they were told in their heathen homes – it was very difficult for them. One of the teachers at Zenka, Alfred Mpofu, was struck by the number of children asking, "What happens after death? Where are the dead?" They could not but wonder. On the one hand there was the teaching at school and on the other the whole medley of ceremony at home; the perennial question, "What is the truth?" would not go away.

There was a happy diversion when the Blood Transfusion Unit came to Ingwenya. Most of the secondary pupils gave blood as also the staff and the workmen, and all were rewarded with a welcome glass of orange juice and sweets. The boys made the most of the occasion. At first they had the idea, or pretended to have, that the teachers wanted to sell their blood at a profit! When Jean went down to their dormitory, where the blood was taken, she got some of them to help her sort the beds, pick up rubbish and generally tidy up. Which they cheerfully did all the while chanting the popular working song, "Si ya sebenza lomama! We are working with Mama!"

When petrol allowed, the teachers might pay a visit to Zenka or Mbuma. There lived little old Mazwabo in a small thatched hut near the hospital. She had been a protegee of Rev James Fraser. A complete heathen whose main interest was beer, she had arrived at his clinic with a sore on her foot which required regular attention. After some weeks of apparently impenetrable deafness to his exhortations she came to church. Soon she exchanged her rags of skins for a dress and Mr Fraser asked her, "Would you like to see yourself in your dress, Mazwabo?" She would, and they went into his house. "There, Mazwabo, look in that long mirror and you will see how nice you look!" She approached the said object somewhat cautiously and then sprang back in terror. "What is that? It's moving!" and she cowered in the

The inimitable Mazwabo.

farthest corner. Assuring her it was no spirit she had glimpsed, Mr Fraser gradually coaxed her to venture near once again. After several abortive attempts she got there. The dress truly was beautiful, she said, but oh, how ugly she was! Perhaps she was, but when she became a Christian she had a bright happy expression that lent beauty to her features.

She was quite a favourite with the hospital staff. Catherine told the visitors from Ingwenya, "She comes into the Out-Patients' Department and grumbles aloud that she never gets a grain of sugar in this terrible place. If she wants a cup of tea she has to take a leaf off a bush and add a little hot water and sugar; we're too mean to give her tea!" Since they all treated her like a queen they found it amusing to hear her daily tirades, delivered with a mischievous glint in her eye.

One holiday she came back with the teachers to Ingwenya for a break. "We brought Mazwabo back here with us. She is lying in the kitchen just now fast asleep. She is quite old but most attractive, very willing to help with any kind of work. But today she asked rather pathetically if she would have to work in the field or the garden and was so relieved when we gave an emphatic 'No!' She is very, very tired."

Back at Mbuma "the inimitable Mazwabo", as Rev Donald MacLean aptly dubbed her, kept everyone in order. Catherine wrote, "Mazwabo is very frail though mentally alert. She has a vegetable plot at the back of the hospital which she attends to whenever she feels fit enough to crawl on all fours to it! We have all enjoyed green mealies, sweet potatoes and tomatoes all home-grown by herself. She is so thrilled to be able to give us something from herself. The apron you sent her is kept for best, worn on Sabbath only."

Widespread changes were envisaged for education – again! Revolutionary might not be too strong a word to apply to it. The Government through Local Community Councils was taking over Primary education which meant that the hold of missions would be relinquished.

Local Community Councils to prepare Africans for democracy had been operating for several years. Under the Community Development Scheme they were responsible for looking after the needs of the community for such amenities as boreholes and roads. By 1965 they

Jean visiting a kraal school in 1966.

A HEART FOR AFRICA

At back, left to right: Margaret MacKenzie and Rhoda Mackay.
Front: Jean, Isobel MacCuish and Marion Graham.

were considered ready gradually to take control of their local primary schools. Since it was the Smith Government that was encouraging this move, the Nationalists were opposed to it fearing a fall in standards.

Primary schools would be staffed by Africans and would have an African head teacher. All teachers must be trained. Every African child was to receive a full primary education. Modern methods would be used in primary schools especially in infant classes and up-to-date equipment and apparatus was to be introduced as far as possible. English was to be the teaching medium throughout. To mark these changes a change in vocabulary was required! Kraal schools became village schools; classes were denominated Grades 1 to 7.

To introduce these changes Margaret MacKenzie and Rhoda Mackay, young teachers recently qualified, ran short courses. At Mbuma they gave lectures and demonstration lessons to the teachers assembled from all over the Mission. Margaret gave an explanation of the New Maths and they showed how basic apparatus could be adapted for various purposes, gave suggestions for making simple aids from such articles as empty cartons, and generally encouraged an interchange of ideas. Mr Mzamo pronounced the venture a great success largely due to the "willingness, ability and competence" of the leaders.

Secondary schools were also to be reorganised. Fifty per cent as against the present twenty per cent of those leaving Primary would enter Secondary school. There would be two distinct types of secondary school: the majority would offer a two-year technical course concentrating on crafts and staffed by indigenous teachers; a smaller number would offer an academic course of four or six years, staffed by suitably trained teachers. Secondary education would thus be in the hands of the Government, including the provision of new buildings and their maintenance.

The Primary school at Ingwenya was thus set to decrease in size as Government guidelines were implemented. It would become purely a day school catering for local children while the Secondary school would expand and become a boarding school offering a four-year course leading to the Cambridge Certificate.

For Jean this meant that, when her present contract came to an end in December, she would be replaced by an African teacher. Mr Nyoni was duly appointed Head Teacher of the Primary school.

During December there were dinners and presentations to mark Jean's retirement after almost 30 years of dedicated service. She had seen the education system grow up from small beginnings largely through the efforts of missions. She was glad that a capable African was taking over responsibility, as was fitting, but felt an inevitable twinge of sadness.

On 7 December 1966 she left for Scotland.

● CHAPTER 15 ●

War of Liberation

JEAN was settled in Edinburgh. Out of the blue she had received a letter from the Admiralty begging her to accept the pension which had been assigned to his dependents by her brother. It had accumulated to a considerable sum and was an embarrassment to them so would she please help them clear their books, as it were, by accepting it? She would and it enabled her to buy a flat in Edinburgh overlooking the Meadows.

In September 1967 she took up a teaching post in the Royal Blind School which she found interesting but very demanding. She always had a story to tell about the children and their resilience – she described the little ones at play as they chased and jostled one another at their favourite game, football; it was wonderful to watch them running pell-mell after the ball which had a tinkling bell inside it. She asked one little fellow from Glasgow how he was getting on. "Fine! I'm daein' whit I'm telt."

Her heart was very much in Africa and she kept in close touch with developments there through letters and visits from Mission folk and their friends to whom her home was something of a mecca. She was delighted to hear of a lively interest in the preaching both among the schoolchildren and the people generally, and that attendance at church was increasing. She was naturally pleased that Dr James Tallach, a nephew of Rev John Tallach, went to serve in the hospital at Mbuma.

She made a point of attending annually the public meeting of Synod to listen to reports from the Mission. Mr Mzamo was present in May 1970 and Mr Ndebele another year. It was a particular pleasure to see her one-time colleagues, Dr and Mrs Macdonald, when they came over from Canada.

When school closed for the summer holidays Jean could no longer resist the lure of Africa and off she went to spend the two months at the Mission. It was while she was there that Abia Sobantu died. Jean wrote, "He was a most intelligent and interesting person and would read with interest any religious books or magazines brought him. . . . His chief delight seemed to be singing the psalms and on one occasion shortly before he died, when we visited him, though he was in great pain he requested Psalm 22 and started it himself, his beautiful voice still sweet though now so weak. . . . His funeral was one of the largest seen in this area. Those present were conscious of an air of triumph and joyousness which could not be hidden even though the loss was so great. One could hardly grieve when it was realised that Abia, now free from all his troubles, is singing in glory the praises, as he so loved to do here, of the One who loved him and gave Himself for him. As one person commented afterwards, 'What a lovely day it was yesterday!' . . . His son, Monde, teaches for us." Hundreds attended his funeral at which there was an air of triumph and joy, many remarking that they were glad to have been there.

The following summer Jean was again in Africa. James Tallach had by this time returned to Scotland and was succeeded by David Ndlovu as builder, interpreter and general overseer of all practical matters from vehicle maintenance to electrical work. Both men took a pride in their work, concerned that buildings should be suitable for their purpose but also as pleasing to the eye as circumstances allowed.

In December Jean resigned from her post in the Royal Blind School, not to retire from work but to return to the Mission. March 1973 found her back in Ingwenya, not this time to teach but as Treasurer of the Mission. In many ways it was a post that suited her admirably. She was ordered and methodical and knew the workings of the Mission inside out. She was meticulous to a fault and would struggle on, if necessary, till she had accounted for every last cent.

She was responsible for keeping track of all money transactions – donations, grants, school fees, transport costs, repairs, equipment. Wages had to be paid to the 115 teachers employed in the three central primary and 21 village schools as also to the eight secondary school teachers. The hospital employed over 30 workers. David Ndlovu had around 40 workmen under his supervision. Catering requirements for all these people and the 200 boarders had to be costed.

Ever adaptable, Jean was able to cope with it and even managed to make her annual Reports interesting – finance with a human face, as it were. She wrote in 1974, "We had a wonderful rainy season and the abundance of rain was most welcome after the previous year of severe drought.

"Despite the fact that all rejoiced to see the rain, it brought its own problems such as swollen rivers and churned-up, pitted roads. Several times one or other of our heavy vehicles was trapped in a mud-hole on the way to or from Mbuma. Vehicles carrying heavy loads of cement, gravel or other building materials were particularly prone to delay. On one occasion at the Bembesi river, on the main road between Bulawayo and Lonely Mine – half-way to Mbuma – there was a long line of vehicles on each side of the river and the police let it be known that the driver of any vehicle attempting to cross the bridge, which was under water, would be heavily fined. We had one vehicle on one side and another one on the other side of the river. It took four hours for the water to subside. . . . Due to increase of labour costs and heavy and frequent repairs on our long-distance lorry and truck, our expenditure on motor vehicles is very heavy indeed. The amount spent last year was $6255.76. . . ." and so she goes on intertwining interesting detail with the financial matters.

The following year's Report mentioned that, since 1973 had been an exceptionally expensive year, "our great resolve in 1974, as far as money was concerned, was to consolidate our financial position. As there was no immediate building programme in view we began some necessary economies, reduced our labour force by half, cut our petrol consumption by one third and scrutinised every small expense. However we record with gratitude to the Most High and to our Mbuma-Zending friends that we received in early June twice the usual donation from Holland, amounting to $43,672. This magnificent sum restored our equilibrium, enabled us to pay off outstanding debts and to face all further necessary expenses with equanimity."

All were saddened to hear of the sudden death in February 1974 of Dr Macdonald, Vancouver. A tribute by fellow-ministers described him as, "Adored by his own and a man of rare qualities . . . cultured, talented, sympathetic and generous. . . . He died as he lived, in peace, leaving a cherished memory worthy of a man of God." Rev A Ndebele said, "Although it is over 26 years since he left the Mission he is still remembered by the older people as a faithful preacher of the gospel. During almost 20 years he tended the sick among neighbouring Europeans as well as Africans and inspired affection and respect among his colleagues on the Mission." Jean, who admired him greatly, wrote, "We heard with a sense of personal loss of the passing of our good friend and former colleague, Dr Macdonald. We knew him as a man of rare integrity and a faithful minister of the gospel." The John Tallach Secondary School inaugurated a Dr Macdonald Arts prize for English and allied subjects – an appropriate memorial.

The school now followed the four-year Cambridge Certificate Course. In 1975 about half the population of Rhodesia were reckoned to be under 17 years of age and almost all were attending primary school; in the whole of Africa only South Africa had a higher proportion of its youngsters in school. Rural schools were gradually passing under the control of the Government. At Ingwenya the local children were increasingly beginning school at age six.

A happy event was the arrival of Rev Donald Ross with his wife, Catherine, and their two little boys. He was inducted in March to the pastoral charge of the growing congregation in Bulawayo. Their home in the city always extended a warm welcome to visitors from the wider Mission area.

On a visit to the Agricultural Show in Bulawayo, while the men admired the cows, Jean and Catherine made for the tapestry stalls and enjoyed a day of carefree leisure. As they were leaving the grounds a long column of the Rhodesian Army marched by, brass band playing, black faces gleaming in the sun. "I love every one of them!" said Jean happily.

A HEART FOR AFRICA

Round house with conical thatched roof.

May 1975 saw the seventieth anniversary of the Mission, and the Mission personnel started to rack their brains as to what might be a suitable way to celebrate it. Various suggestions were put forward and in the end it was Jean's idea that was adopted. They would build a little round house in traditional style with conical thatched roof and pole and dagga wall. The pupils were invited to bring artefacts so that they had a most attractive museum of Matabele culture. Everyone pitched in with enthusiasm and when all was ready the schools Inspector, Mr Phineas Dube, was asked to open it. He had been a pupil at Ingwenya School in the time of Rev John Tallach. At the end of his Primary education his father had expected him to learn a trade but Mr Tallach, recognising his abilities, had with difficulty persuaded his father to allow the lad to continue his academic education. At the opening he had interesting things to say about his days at Ingwenya.

Jean was unable to stay for the opening of the Craft House. She had been having trouble with her eyesight and in early 1975 she was forced to go home for surgery, disappointed that she could not finish her term. Mr Ross was to take over from Jean until someone would come forward to replace her.

He and Catherine ran her to the airport and after goodbyes she got on to the plane and they waited ready to wave her off. They waited. And waited. Why was the plane not moving? Now the boarding platform was being wheeled back into position. The door opened. Jean emerged with the Captain's arm around her shoulder; together they descended the steps and walked towards the barrier talking together. "What's wrong? Is she ill?" they wondered. Then over the tannoy; "Would Rev Donald Ross come on to the tarmac to meet the Captain?" As he reached them Jean handed him a little bag of money – the petty cash! She had meant to give it to him on leaving the office but had inadvertently put it in her bag. Chatting animatedly she and the Captain turned back to the plane, he completely charmed by her – so said Catherine. With a cheerful wave she stepped inside and was soon on her way to "bonnie Scotland".

Since there was no response to an advertisement for the post of treasurer Jean returned in October 1976 to a period of escalating political tension though on the surface all was calm.

The sanctions imposed by Britain against the rebel regime of Ian Smith after UDI had at first little apparent effect on the country at large. Factories continued to produce goods and the shops were as full as ever. The Nationalist movement had continued to grow, quietly for the most part, though there were sporadic incidents during the late 1960s and early 1970s, and gradually shortages made themselves felt. Consultations between Ian Smith and Joshua Nkomo to explore the possibility of forming a constitution acceptable to both Africans and white Rhodesians had broken down.

By 1976 the Nationalist movement was gathering momentum; the freedom fighters or terrorists, depending on who was speaking – were more active and bold. Boys from some schools were slipping over the border to join the amalwecatsha, as they were called in Ndebele, and while none did so from Ingwenya and the school was running smoothly, yet there was unrest. After one holiday some pupils did not return to school; their parents were threatened with death if their children did so. Their places were taken by those from schools that had closed and the stories they had to tell were disturbing; the grandfather of one of the girls was thrown on to a bonfire of schoolbooks and shot. Hearing reports of such wanton cruelty, the youngsters in Ingwenya school felt privileged and worked hard. Pupils lost fathers, brothers, uncles and other relatives; scarcely a family in the country but was visited by death.

One promising feature was the call on more than one occasion by the President, Hon John Wrathall, for a Day of Prayer. At Ingwenya, school was closed early and a service was held at noon attended by children, teachers and the local people.

Two elders at Zenka:
E P Mnkandla (left) and Magaya Ncube.

There was indiscriminate murder and torture of civilians of all races but it was the ordinary African who suffered most. When dip-tanks were closed, disease wrought havoc among the cattle, the main source of his income, so he was left in poverty. Without cattle he could not plough his fields; ensuing hunger and malnutrition were invariably accompanied by disease. Closing down of medical facilities meant a rise in infant mortality. Stores were robbed and subsequently abandoned. Teachers, health workers and thousands of employees were robbed of their livelihood as hospitals, schools, stores and industries were forced to close.

Schools were being attacked by the amalwecatsha as a protest against the Government. They set fire to mission schools and destroyed books and furniture, though it was the schools as such rather than the missions that were their particular target. Teachers were beaten, mutilated, clubbed to death or even burnt alive. The school buildings at Simba were set ablaze and the children and teachers warned that they would be killed if they tried to put out the fire. A man was ordered to dig his own grave. Jean wrote, "Schools three miles from Zenka were closed and the Zenka teacher reports that the children are now afraid to come to school and, if they come, they come late with no pencils or books;" they were afraid of meeting the amalwecatsha.

An embargo on travelling in the Shangani area meant that the European staff especially were restricted to Ingwenya and the occasional trip to town. Tension was high in the townships. In Bulawayo, a centre of strife, many victims were caught in the crossfire between the Security Forces and insurgents.

Many missions were withdrawing their personnel. Members of the Foreign Missions Committee back in Scotland met officials of the Foreign and Commonwealth Office in London who warned that a serious situation was inevitable in Rhodesia within two years. It was made clear that, should trouble arise, the British government would not give assistance, within Rhodesia, to British subjects though emergency help from outwith the border might be available. This information was relayed to the European staff, who indicated that they had at the moment no intention of leaving the Mission but were relying on the Most High to preserve and guide them.

The Mission in Rhodesia pursued its primary aim of evangelising, with education and medicine as ancillary enterprises. All members of staff therefore avoided involvement in politics, though naturally they had their various opinions about the situation.

A message of encouragement from the home Church concluded, "The Synod would assure you all that you are constantly remembered at a Throne of Grace, where we plead for your preservation from all harm and seek that you may be upheld in your Christian profession so that, in the midst of every trial, you may enjoy the consolations of the everlasting gospel. 'The eternal God is thy refuge and underneath are the everlasting arms.'"

Nkai Tribal Trust Land, in which Mbuma and Zenka were situated, was particularly vulnerable to attack by the amalwecatsha as it was part of the war zone, where Nationalist feeling was strong. It was under martial law and a curfew was imposed. Amalwecatsha forces were especially active near Mbuma, the most vulnerable of the

Mission stations, isolated as it was. Numerous incidents took place within walking distance of the hospital.

Not long after Jean's return they heard of the murder in that area of a Roman Catholic bishop, a priest and a nun. In early June 1977 a European forester was shot three miles from Mbuma and his body mutilated. About two weeks later a band of amalwecatsha marched into St Paul's, a German Roman Catholic hospital to the west of Mbuma. Bursting into the wards they ordered the doctor and two nuns out into the yard and shot them. Dr Decker had built up the hospital from nothing through 27 years of dedicated work and as one of her clinics was a mere 12 miles from Mbuma she was known to some of the staff there.

On 13 June 1977 shortly after midnight the staff on duty at Mbuma were visited by armed amalwecatsha who questioned them for an hour about the hospital and especially about the movements of the European workers. Who were on the staff? When were they on duty? Did they hold clinics? Where? When? As suddenly and quietly as they had appeared they slipped away. When the incident was reported to the District Commissioner at Nkai his advice was, "Leave! You must go by Friday at the very latest. Your safety cannot be guaranteed. And besides, it's safer for the Africans if there are no Europeans with them."

A frenzy of packing followed. Sisters Jocelyn Cox, Jantien van Saane and Cathie Ann Turner arranged for the convalescent patients to be sent home immediately. The seriously ill were transferred to Bulawayo. The hospital contained valuable equipment – refrigerators, steel cupboards, x-ray machines, delicate surgical instruments and smaller but no less essential items. James Mpofu, the Mission carpenter set to and made crates while Neil Murray and David Ndlovu saw to the packing. The goods were taken to Bulawayo by lorry and stored safely with the Black Cat Storage Company. The whole business of dismantling the hospital and dispersing the contents of the houses was wearying and sad for all, both those going and those staying.

The refugees climbed on to the Mission lorry which drove out of the south gate and made for Ingwenya. Cathie Ann remembered, "Jean was a tower of strength to us during that difficult time." David

Ndlovu whose home was in that area said, "They got out just in time, no more; just at the right time." The hospital was closed for almost four years.

A few months later Mbuma School was targeted. The amalwecatsha ordered the children out before torching the building. They then helped themselves to medicines from the hospital but while they caused considerable damage they did not destroy the buildings. Soon all mission schools in the Zenka and Mbuma areas were closed.

In her report for that year Jean touched on the tensions of the past months but added, "During the year we have often thought of the verse, 'He stayeth His rough wind in the day of the east wind.' Financially we have never been so well off as we have been during the past year. . . . It was a singular mercy – though I hope at all times we are punctilious in the expenditure of mission funds – not to have the added anxiety of trying to make ends meet in those days of political instability. Most of the money came from our generous Dutch friends, whom we cannot thank too warmly for the wonderful kindness."

At Ingwenya they were advised by Chief Ndiweni to erect a security fence which David Ndlovu immediately arranged. It was a double fence, the inner one eight feet high with a six-foot gap between it and an outer one, four feet high, which was designed to keep animals away from the inner fence. At the red-brick gateway was the gatehouse from which the Mission was guarded by day and night. Three men kept watch in turn patrolling the fence and checking everyone in and out. Security lighting and an alarm system were installed.

David wrote, "We have done what we can as men to stop enemies marching in. Let us look past this man-made fence and look to Him who is a wall of fire and ask Him to build us a fence of fire! He can do for us those things we cannot do for ourselves."

The staff were issued with revolvers and had regular target practice which, though it underlined the precarious situation in which the Mission operated, had its more light-hearted moments. Some of the learners proved themselves crack shots when the target was an inanimate sitting duck but how they would react in a real emergency

Mr P Ndebele, elder, Zenka, with Jean Nicolson shortly before his death in 1979.

they were not sure. Would they really grab their weapons and use them? One said she would, without hesitation, if attacked. Katie said emphatically she would not. Jean said she would – in principle anyway.

The alarm system was centred in Jean's house. One evening came the warning, that "the army was hunting down a band of terrorists amalwecatsha who were reported to be approaching Ingwenya." Immediately she alerted the others. One by one, silently, they arrived at her house where in darkness they waited . . . . With welcome morning light the danger had passed. The sun shone, morning voices called out greetings and with hearts full of gratitude for divine protection they took up the duties of a new day.

They were deeply saddened by news of the massacre at Elim Mission near Umtali the following June, when 13 people, including three young children and a baby, were brutally killed in a revenge attack for the security forces having killed a band of amalwecatsha. The teachers and their families were driven from their homes at gun-point, shot and mutilated. The staff at Ingwenya knew some of them.

In 1979 the War of Liberation was at its height. Travel in any form was a risk to one's life. Wherever they went, the driver or his companion had a loaded rifle at the ready. Incidents of pointless cruelty were innumerable. A deacon at Simba suffered severely at the hands of the security forces. His son of 13 years was shot dead at his side. He himself was put under detention and came home semi-blinded. At Donsa School a young teacher, a former head girl of the John Tallach Secondary School was flogged almost to death; and after

Rev B B Dube (left) with Rev P Mzamo, Rev A Ndebele and Rev D A Ross, at Mr Dube's induction to the Zenka congregation.

piling up the school books and furniture at gun point, she was forced to look on while they shot and killed the local Headman's son. His body was then thrown on the pyre of books and furniture.

Large schools, such as Zenka School, with five or six hundred pupils were shut down at the command of amalwecatsha. More than 500 African schools with 40 mission hospitals and clinics were closed. This included all those in the Zenka and Mbuma areas though the Church remained fairly active. Elders such as David Ndlovu showed outstanding courage in keeping services regularly. When armed men suddenly appeared at the door of the church while he was preaching, he knelt down and prayed. He then invited them to lay their weapons at their feet and listen to the sermon. They did.

An occasion full of promise was the induction in October 1978 of Rev B B Dube to the charge of Zenka church. Because of the volatile situation in Shangani it was decided to hold the service at Ingwenya and by the previous evening a large crowd had gathered. The service took place the following morning and after a meal all left early in order to reach home before curfew. An elder, Elisha Mkandla, came from his home at Katasa near Zenka although he was nearly a hundred years old and it was remarked that he looked noticeably happy and content. It was his last day on earth. That night he passed away in the home of William Mpofu. The last of the old elders, he was described as a man "mighty in prayer".

A HEART FOR AFRICA

It was encouraging to have young Africans coming forward for the work of the ministry. Revs Alfred Mpofu and Z Mazvabo would be soon settled in congregations.

In spite of the general unrest and turmoil the situation remained relatively calm at Ingwenya. It was one of only five country schools to remain open. When, towards the end of 1979, a neighbouring school was attacked and two girls were killed – one a former Ingwenya pupil – the staff began to wonder how much longer they could continue. David Livingstone School, a few miles away, had to close for a time.

Thousands were moved from Tribal Trust Lands to the cities for safety. Some of the country folk – the older people especially – were utterly confused, at a loss to understand what was going on and those who could not read had difficulty knowing what exactly the trouble was all about.

Jean used to encourage perplexed ones, often quoting Habakkuk, "Although the fig tree shall not blossom, neither shall fruit be in the vines; the labour of the olive tree shall fail, and the fields shall yield no meat; the flock shall be cut of from the fold, and there shall be no herd in the stalls: yet I will rejoice in the LORD, I will joy in the God of my salvation."

By 1979 everyone was weary of the strife and longing for a settlement. A ceasefire was announced and at a conference in Lancaster House it was agreed to hold free and fair elections in three months' time. It would be one man, one vote. All, African and European, would vote to form a government. The Lancaster House Agreement thus marked the end of the seven-year War of Liberation. Elections towards the end of February 1980 duly returned a majority black Government.

At Ingwenya the elections caused no great excitement; "We took our few 18-year-olds to vote at the local polling booth," reported Marion, "and we were interested to meet a real live Scottish "Bobby"! He came for a short visit to the school and spoke to our senior pupils for a few minutes. This was the real highlight of the elections as far as we were concerned!"

April 18, Independence Day, was memorable. The Union Jack was taken down and the colours of the now legally independent

Zimbabwe were raised amid general elation and celebration. Almost 90 years of white rule had come to an end. After the thousands of civilian deaths since U.D.I., among them 38 missionaries, hopes were high for a multi-racial state. With its rich untapped mineral resources, immense agricultural potential and possibilities for tourism, the future looked bright.

Jean's term of service came to an end just as Zimbabwe had become independent and its reconstruction programme was due to get underway.

Her final Report ended, "We wish to record our gratitude to all the friends in many countries who have surrounded us with prayer, and no doubt, under the Most High, these prayers have been effectual in the preservation of our people, throughout the years of war."

She flew home on 19 May 1980. At the Synod, meeting in Glasgow at that time, acknowledgement was made of her fine contribution to the work in Africa. "Our friend, Miss Jean Nicolson, is now retiring from service on the Church's Mission in Zimbabwe. Her gracious character and example earned the highest esteem and respect from old and young among Africans and Europeans. Her sterling qualities as a teacher and Headmistress in the Mission School during many years contributed to the stability of the Mission and to the high standard of education given to the African pupils. This was recognised by the African Education Department over the years."

Mr Ndebele said; "It would be superfluous for me to say that we miss Miss Nicolson in Zimbabwe, as such follows without saying. But at the same time we cannot grudge her a rest after years of labour in the African sun. We know she loved the Africans; she loved her work and above all she had a mind to work in Africa. It is the Lord alone who can give her a sense of satisfaction as she looks as far back as 1933 in Ingwenya, with her late co-workers Revs John Tallach and Dr Macdonald, together with a host of Africans who loved the Lord in sincerity."

Her own verdict on her long years among these courteous, loveable people? "I'd live it all over again!"

CHAPTER 16

Final Years

HOME was a flat in Warrander Park Terrace, Edinburgh, a row of solid stone-built tenements. She was "one stair up" and she skipped smartly up those steps till into her nineties. The large, bright sitting-room was attractively and comfortably furnished, with a bay window which looked on to the stately trees and busy pathways of the Meadows.

She used her home well and seldom, if ever, a week passed that she did not have someone to stay or for a meal. She maintained good

Jean Nicolson in her flat in Warrander Park Terrace, Edinburgh.

relations with her Mission colleagues, African and European, over a period of 50 years and when she retired to Edinburgh they were her most frequent visitors. She had a wide circle of friends besides – old and new, in both senses of these words! She had a special rapport with the young; her home was open to students in Edinburgh who came to her church – and others – and she by no means expected that they should always want to visit "an old lady". She was not dependent on them and expected that they would in time find friends of their own.

She greatly appreciated the preaching of the ministers who served the church in Gilmore Place – in succession Revs Donald Campbell, Angus Morrison, Donald B Macleod and Hugh Cartwright – and was glad of the opportunity to support other efforts at spreading the gospel. She attended meetings of the Trinitarian Bible Society and the Scottish Reformation Society. One letter described a meeting of the Scottish Reformed Conference. At lunch one of the speakers shared her table. "Mr Marshall asked about the Mission and said to my astonishment, 'Is that where Mr Ndebele is?' 'Have you met him?' 'No, but I used to get the *Free Presbyterian Magazine* and saw his name.' It was very interesting to chat."

As she was interested in art she enjoyed visiting the art galleries and museums that Edinburgh had to offer. She had some very pleasing pictures – usually of scenes with an element of human interest. Cathie Ann remembers, "One Saturday afternoon she went with me to a small gallery where my sister had an exhibition of her paintings. She noticed some paintings of flowers from the Arizona desert. The person in charge of the gallery was so impressed with her knowledge and, when my sister went in later, he told her all about this lady who knew so much about the flowers and at such a remarkable age! I am sure she would have liked to have had a garden of her own."

She was not particularly interested in domestic matters. Since her mother had always seen to the household affairs Jean had no need to learn and, after her mother's death, there was always a well-trained housekeeper to see to the cooking and other tasks. However she was as competent as she needed to be and invariably set before her guests a delightful meal.

As a guest she was easy to please, appreciating whatever was provided. She ate fairly abstemiously and remained slim and erect, and active, all her days. She was also considerate, always punctual about any outings that were arranged. Usually she would retire about 10 o'clock announcing in lighted-hearted fashion, "Well, dears, I think I'll 'op it. When do you want me up for breakfast?" and next morning she would appear at the appointed minute.

She was punctilious about the niceties, unfailingly writing a "thank-you" letter on her return

Handing over the administration at Ingwenya to William Campbell.

home recounting any amusing incident or interesting encounter en route. She kept up a wide correspondence, her letters for the most part in newsy, chatty style.

She had been succeeded as administrator at Ingwenya by William Campbell and a few months after retiring she concluded a letter to him, "My thoughts are continually of the Mission, and I have been thinking of the text my Mother quoted with great earnestness, when she was ill at Ingwenya; Isaiah 62 verses 6 & 7; 'Ye that make mention of the Lord, keep not silence . . . till He make Jerusalem a praise in the earth.' Please remember me to all, black and white. A tall order! Warm regards. . . ."

By the following September she was in Africa relieving him for six weeks and again in April 1983 when he went on leave for six months. It was to a deteriorating political situation. The peace brokered in 1980 had proved to be simply a pause for breath. The

African leaders were jockeying for power among themselves. Tribal loyalties were strong and there was a growing division between the majority Shona owing allegiance to Robert Mugabe and the Matabele with Joshua Nkomo at their head. Adding to the unrest was the presence of young men suddenly idle after the activity of the bush and with their weapons still at hand. They roamed the country harassing the people while lawlessness and violence, lootings, murders and atrocities went unchecked.

The bright promise of the early months of the new Zimbabwe had given way before an economic downturn, and food and fuel were in short supply. As before, it was the civilian population who suffered. Dissidents and army deserters descended on the kraals demanding food, money and shelter at gunpoint; in turn the security forces came looking for dissidents, questioning the locals and dealing ruthlessly with any who failed to report their presence. On the other hand, if they were to report them, the insurgents would show no mercy.

This second wave of disturbance was centred in Matabeleland with much of the activity concentrated in the Nkai area, where

Ministers of the Zimbabwe Presbytery. Left to right: Rev B B Dube, Rev P Mzamo, Rev A Ndebele, Rev Dr J R Tallach, Rev A Mpofu, Rev Z Mazvabo. Photo taken in the early 1980s.

A HEART FOR AFRICA

Mugabe's Fifth Brigade was hunting down Nkomo's followers. A troop of soldiers turned up at Zenka one Sabbath morning just as the people were beginning to gather for church. When the "bell" began its slow rhythmic beat they thought it was a signal to dissidents and grew edgy. Three lads, pupils of the school, were shot dead. A member of the congregation, John Dube, was killed a week later leaving a widow with three children. Such were everyday incidents – a woman was shot simply for cooking food to celebrate Independence Day.

The hospital had been reopened in March 1981. For a while all went well but dissidents were operating in the vicinity and Dr Tallach received a letter threatening the European staff with death if they did not leave. The authorities at Nkai thought it likely that the threats would be carried out and strongly advised them to go. There was a scramble to pack. Seven African nurse aids and an ambulance driver volunteered to remain. With the insurgents on their heels the fugitives found themselves a place among the goods on the lorry and made off, Jessie Coote perched on top of a fridge calmly knitting!

While the others went home she remained at Ingwenya from whence she kept a general oversight of the situation at Mbuma and, by the time Jean arrived, had established herself as a very helpful school nurse.

Hostilities intensified. Up to 20,000 men, women and children were maimed and killed in the early years of the continuing conflict. The armed struggle between the army and Nkomo's men was to continue till 1986 when the Declaration of Unity brought about a gradual peace. Finally, in July 1988 there was an Agreement between Mugabe and Nkomo following an amnesty to the dissidents on laying down their arms.

In these circumstances the Missionary Aviation Fellowship plane was a boon for travelling to Mbuma and during the troubles the missionaries were grateful for the cheerful efficiency of their pilots. When William returned in October Jean went home to Edinburgh. This was her final working visit in Zimbabwe!

Like all those on the Mission Jean had been well aware of the generous contribution made by the hundreds of supporters in

Holland. Each year there was a large gathering and often a minister from Scotland or Africa was invited to address it. Jean attended the 1982 meeting at Utrecht. That springtime there was a crowd of 7,500 and they came from all over Holland. Those from Staphorstin were colourful in their distinctive dress and others wore conventional Dutch national costume with broad white linen hats. The singing by such a throng was memorable.

During these years of comparative leisure Jean enjoyed travel. She was entertained to a cruise to Norway but declined the offer of a trip by yacht to St Kilda. While in the Lake District Jean and some of her Mission friends visited Wordsworth's cottage in Grasmere; they also visited art galleries and some bought paintings. Another year they were in Aberystwyth. There were visits to Orkney and Shetland as well as further afield to Canada.

Her relatives meant a lot to Jean and she made a point of keeping in touch. Several of them came from Canada and the States to visit her. These cousins admired and loved Jean and made every effort to maintain the family links which she greatly appreciated. Letters contained references to them: "I had a little cousin of mine with me, Lesle Buch. She was one of the party with her grandfather and grandmother when we met in Inverness. She is a pilot with United Airways – had flown over to London privately."

John and Nancy Creech came several times; John was a nephew of little Grace who had so charmed Jean's father when he arrived in San Francisco. A cousin from the States, Chris MacAskill, visited her and subsequently wrote, "She is one of the finest and most interesting people I've ever known, and she is sharp and clear at the age of ninety. When she heard we were coming to visit she walked the twenty-minute walk in blustery weather to the store to buy fresh strawberries, trout, and vegetables so she could prepare a proper dinner. Then she insisted on washing the dishes saying with a smile, 'They're my dishes!'"

In 1991 with two friends she made a short visit to Ingwenya taking the long journey in her stride, as it were. In the darkness of night the plane started juddering and dropping, juddering and dropping. Jean, sitting upright apparently asleep, opened her eyes, said, "Just turbulence," and resumed her sleep.

Marion, Etta, Katie and Ishbel were at Ingwenya. It felt like old times. The local people were overjoyed to see her. Much to Jean's amusement a former pupil she met in Bulawayo greeted her with unconcealed astonishment, "You are still alive? Ah, ah!"

One afternoon three men came walking purposefully into the compound, wheeled as one through the gateway to Marion's house and sat down to talk animatedly with Jean round the dining-room table. One was Sipho Nxusani, known to Jean first as a little boy and latterly as the headmaster of Cameron School, about ten miles from Ingwenya.

It was satisfying to find Africans working in posts that were previously the preserve of white people. A small African middle class had emerged. In town Jean noticed two little 10-year-olds, hand in hand in Haddon and Sly, one black, one white – a welcome sight. And in church she was pleased to see how smartly dressed the people were. There was something else new – the sight of poverty-stricken white people.

There were shortages in many areas. The near impossibility of replacing outworn vehicles and the difficulty in obtaining spare parts,

Etta MacLennan. The bags in the background probably contain mealie-meal.

together with scarcity of petrol, had repercussions throughout the whole economy and impacted on daily life at all levels. Breakdowns and accidents were all too frequent.

The teachers took their visitors a run to Matopo Hills near Bulawayo and savoured the sense of calm and space as they stood on World's View. Smooth rounded rocks balanced impossibly on one another, shy lizards appearing from a nook and as quickly disappearing. On the way back they had the inevitable breakdown and the patient wait till someone should hap along and do a very temporary repair or take a message to a source of help.

Jean was anxious to see friends in Zenka and Mbuma so off went the car with its five occupants. After some miles it staggered to a halt. Katie got out without a word, opened the bonnet, lifted a rod, smack! and got back into the car. Off it went. For a bit. Again the engine petered out. Out got Katie. Smack! and off it went. Katie was not known for being specially insightful about cars. Etta asked, "What's the trouble?" "I don't know," owned Katie, "but one time I just tried giving it a whack and it worked so that's what I always do."

Rocks at Matopo Hills.

A HEART FOR AFRICA

Communion services were being held at Zenka and a large crowd had gathered. At Mbuma they were guests of Neil and Cathie Ann Murray. At daybreak girls in single file, bundles on heads, walking off to work, calling to one another in happy morning voices; breakfast on the verandah, looking over the dainty trees with sunlight filtering through; a braai in Jessie's garden, and a visit to a huge baobab tree – all were memories to treasure. There was a visit to a mother-and-toddler clinic in the large well-run hospital. A sad aspect was the prevalence of HIV and its consequences socially with a generation seemingly being decimated.

A baobab – 80ft in circumference. Its size can be judged by the three people standing at the base, one of whom is Norman Miller.

Three weeks passed quickly. Back in Edinburgh Jean wrote, "It seems like a dream to be back in the old surroundings so quickly. A chilly wind blows today, and yet I can transport myself quite quickly in imagination to the dusty heat of Zimbabwe.

"I really enjoyed the holiday very much. It was most refreshing and I enjoyed the company – camaraderie – which I lack here. I do regret not having made the effort to see Ma Nyati, Simon Moyo's widow. She is a very sweet, friendly person."

One aspect of retirement she greatly valued was having more time to read. She had been a reader all her life and read mainly, but not exclusively, religious books for she was also interested in secular history and biography. Missionaries, unsurprisingly, featured in her reading. She was probably quite an expert in the general history of

Africa and its evangelisation. She was glad when the Banner of Truth Trust began to publish Puritan works and many of these adorned her bookshelves. If she discovered an interesting book she would buy a few and send them off to friends. She read a quality newspaper and listened to the radio but did not like television.

Snippets from her letters indicate what she was currently reading; "I have just reread *Another Hand on Mine* for the third time! . . . I do feel the better of our lovely holiday!"

"Here is the promised book at long last. As you can see it is really a life of Stewart; he was the founder of Lovedale. He, as you will see, was an extraordinary man – larger than life."

"Here is *Dan Crawford*. I enjoyed it immensely, on a second reading. I should love to get a copy of Arnot who preceded Dan Crawford in Mushdi's kingdom. It is most interesting how savage minds and hearts appreciated the moral worth of those early missionaries although they did not appreciate the spiritual aspect."

"In the morning the text was from 1 Corinthians 11, verses 24 & 25. He referred to Charles Simeon's quandary when he went as a student to Cambridge in 1779 and discovered he was expected to take communion, knowing that he was unconverted, and how he set to to study the Scriptures and give himself to prayer with the result that he was converted before the solemn occasion. I have Simeon's biography and read it again, at least that part of it. One point that helped Simeon was a quotation from a minister of that time, that the Jews knew what it meant when they were to put their hands on the head of the sacrifice."

"I did enjoy reading *Fear no Foe*. It is a charming book."

"Cathie Ann returned John's book, *Give Me That Joy!* I have not read it as yet."

Cathie Ann remembers, "She always enjoyed a walk over to the Christian Bookroom on Forrest Road and having a chat with the young men there. She loved buying missionary books and sharing them with us. I remember when I went to the Mission first, she encouraged me to buy George Muller's book.

"She was indeed a lively personality. I was thinking the other day how she loved coming over and giving Neil a tin filled with rock buns, as she knew how he relished them. She was so appreciative of any small jobs he would do for her. She was so independent and would move pieces of furniture; then Neil would be chiding her for having done so!"

She was a good conversationalist and in company Jean spoke, others listened. Having travelled in Canada and America she was well-informed in a general way and so was an interesting companion. She observed people and events and places with a keen eye, and since she had a good memory, she was never short of an anecdote.

She was asked to keep the Church in general up-to-date with Mission developments through its Magazine so each month it carried Mission News. She was most grateful to those in the field who sent items she could incorporate in the articles. Another writing development and one which brought the Mission alive to many was the short series of sketches she wrote of Africans – MaDonsa, MaNgwenya, Paul Magaya and others. These old Christians she revered greatly.

A series she wrote on John Radasi led to the suggestion that she write a book about him for young people. So the early 1990s saw her embarking on this. It was quite an undertaking for so much regarding him was unknown or lost. Also she felt that if she had attempted it when she was younger she would have managed it so much more easily. However she would do what she could and *John Boyana Radasi* was duly published with its interesting photographs.

In 1993 the Church celebrated its centenary in Edinburgh and several Africans came over from Zimbabwe. Talks covering various aspects of the Church's witness included one by Rev Petros Mzamo on the work in Zimbabwe. After the meetings the delegates travelled in Scotland. Some had their first experience of sailing as they crossed the Minch to the Hebrides. Rev A Ndebele saw for the first time sheep being sheared. On a visit to a West Highland home two of the gentlemen could not conceal their vexation on seeing a garden hose left running – a reckless waste of water! "After dinner," their host told them, "I'll show you where it comes from," and as they gazed at the loch in the hills they said in wonder, "And all that for you alone!"

Overleaf: "African Mission News" which appeared in the **Free Presbyterian Magazine** *of September 1997.*

African Mission News

ZIMBABWE

AT **Ingwenya** it is good that at last they have the telephone system installed. It is expected that Mbuma Mission will soon have an equally good service, as the telephone engineers are hard at work there. The staff at Mbuma were in a very isolated situation when their radio communication system was out of order.

The water shortage situation at Ingwenya has eased because of the extra water being now piped from the nearby dam. Meantime, it is being used for washing clothes and cleaning generally, but it is hoped that it will eventually be put through a purifying process and be suitable for all purposes.

Miss Marion Graham is in Scotland on furlough, and we hope she will have a refreshing holiday. Miss Etta MacLennan will be leaving for Zimbabwe about the end of August, if all is well, to give assistance in the John Tallach School while Miss Graham is on holiday.

It was interesting to have news of the Mission and to know that the Rev A. B. Ndebele is in much better health. Ma Donsa, who is probably the oldest member in the Ingwenya congregation, is not able to attend church as regularly as before. Ma Donsa is usually associated with the memory of her grandmother, Ma Mlotshwa, one of the chief wives of the last king of the Matabele, Lobengula. I recollect that Ma Mlotshwa came in contact with our Church when on one occasion, many years ago, she was out walking near her home at Libeni. She came across a small gospel meeting held by one of our elders, and she stopped to listen. After that she made a point of attending these meetings, and also began to attend church. Then she was converted. From being a rather wild, intemperate old lady she became a fine Christian and lived to a good old age. Her last words were, "Receive thou me, O Lord of Glory."

There are five young people from Scotland at present on holiday at Ingwenya, all wishing to be as useful as possible. It is very cheering and helpful for the staff to have them there.

From Mbuma a friend writes: "There was a sad death one night recently. A three year old boy found something to drink in a cupboard at home, which he may have thought was milk, but turned out to be poison from the root of a tree. No doubt there was some specific use for it in the home. He died soon after his arrival in hospital.

"Miss Lia Terlou is making plans for her furlough. She hopes to accompany her parents to Scotland. . . We were hoping we would get a relief nurse in her place but so far nobody is forthcoming. They are very busy in Sengera [Kenya] and need all the hands they have."   *J. N.*

JOHN BOYANA RADASI

Missionary to Zimbabwe

Jean Nicolson

Jean went to see them off at the airport; they were as happy and as excited as schoolboys going home for the holidays, laughing, joking, filling in forms, grabbing trolleys and piling them high – having evidently found the shops!

December 1994 was the ninetieth anniversary of the arrival of John Radasi in Africa to start mission work and the happy decision was taken to invite Jean to present the prizes that year. Notice was given that Miss Nicolson was expected at the prize-giving. Parents arrived by bus, car and foot, a huge gathering, on Open Day, Saturday, 5 November. The hall could not hold them all but a loudspeaker system had been recently installed so that those outside could hear proceedings. There were displays of sewing, woodwork and art and the singing club led by James Mpofu displayed their skills. Jean gave the address; her reminiscences of the early days were fascinating, especially for those whose grandparents had been among her pupils. The audience was entranced. Gales of laughter greeted the stories of the trials and tribulations of those long-ago times. She told of how the grandfather of James Mpofu, one of their teachers, had persuaded a missionary to give him a Bible and asked, "What are these little black ants on the pages?" Then she went on to speak of more serious and abiding matters, mentioning some of the remarkable conversions of those days. When she asked if it was time to stop there were cries of "Go on!"

She concluded, "I feel honoured to have known these people – Mr Patrick Mzamo, Mr Philemon Ndebele and many others. Rev J B Radasi and these godly people laid the foundation of the Mission with Rev John Tallach and Dr Macdonald. They were truthful and honest, kind and loving. Some could not read or write. Some were very poor, had no shoes on their feet, but these people were a blessing in their own generation. They tried to bring others to the Lord Jesus and what does God say of them? He says they will shine as the stars for ever and ever."

Afterwards, as they made their way to the dining-room for refreshments, she was mobbed by well-wishers. Marion pronounced the day a complete success and Jean "the best guest speaker we've ever had – this is the general opinion! The children were riveted by her stories and would have listened for as long as she cared to talk! Clementine Radasi, who is a Form 2 pupil and the great-grand-daughter of the founder, presented flowers to Jean. Since school closed I had a visit from Mildred, the granddaughter of J B Radasi and his first wife, Annie, and now her youngest daughter is coming to Form 1 next year. So the link is being maintained."

Old friends came to visit, among them MaNdiweni, sister-in-law of Chief Kayisa, and there was much reminiscing. Two old ladies she missed especially were Mrs Maseko and Mrs Sithole, sisters-in-law who had lived beside each other. On one

A photo of Mrs Macdonald (widow of the Rev Roderick Macdonald), taken in Vancouver in 1994 – "as spirited and energetic (within her limits) as ever and interested in all the 'Mission' activities."

occasion after comments were made in a sermon about people being late for church Jean had noticed the two arriving an hour early – they had no clock of course – and called them over to her house. After that they often found their way down to the Mission for a cup of tea and a chat. Not being used to sitting on chairs they preferred to sit out on the verandah and picnic there! They were very poor as they were both widows but whenever possible they would bring a few eggs or, after harvest, a few green mealies.

A trip to Mbuma by MAF plane provided a piquant contrast where matron Margaret Macaskill showed her round the up-to-date, well-equipped hospital.

At Ingwenya Rev A Ndebele often had up to a thousand to preach to and door collections showed that the people were becoming more aware of their responsibilities. More men were coming than formerly. Katie and Mr Teus Benschop from Holland were soon to be engaged in revising the Ndebele Bible with the help of Mr N Mpofu, Mr B Mziya and Mr E Manzini – a considerable undertaking.

Marion Graham, headmistress of the John Tallach Secondary School.

There were now 600 secondary school pupils with about 40 teaching and ancillary staff under Marion as headmistress. Ten blind pupils had a specially equipped resource room and there was a primary school for local children. Norma MacLean, qualified in business studies, had recently arrived. She would introduce a whole new vocabulary into the pupils' speech – photocopiers, fax machines, internet. . . .

Jean must have gone back in mind to her first visit to the Mission. A letter suggests a nostalgic mood; "On Friday I went for a walk in the morning with Mar up to the cemetery with many thoughts. Mr Ndebele called later. When we spoke of the past his eyes filled with tears. He is much thinner but is much troubled with his back. He was asking warmly for everyone. Saturday – we sat around, I hardly realising I was at Ingwenya! . . . Rev Ndebele took the service. I could hear only a little but it was good to be there. In the evening English service the singing was beautiful, the boys harmonising. It was good to shake hands with Cecil Sobantu, Monde, Manzini; Paul Moyo was interpreting. Quite a number of women came forward including Dinah Manzini."

A HEART FOR AFRICA

Jean often reverted in thought to the early days. In some ways they were the happiest – the freshness of youth, the clarity of purpose, the sense of achievement with discernible results; even the make-shift improvisation took on a halo in the glow of hindsight. And now the fruit of labours past was to be seen in the new buildings, expansion of opportunity, lives influenced. And there were results spiritually, some they knew about, others not yet known to them.

This was Jean's farewell to the Mission. Back in Edinburgh her life continued on its old tenor, writing

Rev D B Macleod (1929-1995).

"Mission News" and sketches of noteworthy African Christians and entertaining friends. In 1995 her minister and friend, Rev D B Macleod, died suddenly. He had taken a keen interest in the Mission and was, Jean wrote, "a very gentle pastor and anxious to help at all times, as well as being a faithful preacher of the gospel."

Her friend Mrs Turner lived nearby and she was glad when her daughter Cathie Ann with her husband came to stay with her. Jean had known them on the Mission and they often popped in to see her. Cathie Ann remembers, "She was very interested in Simon, the young boy who lived downstairs from her. He and his mother would sometimes visit her and she would advise his mother to take him to church and teach him the Ten Commandments. Any time I meet her they speak about her."

She had a general concern for her neighbours. One weekend when she was at communion services in Glasgow, she had a compelling urge to see an elderly frail lady who lived on her stair. She felt she ought to have checked up on her before she left home. Helen MacLean drove her all the way back on the Saturday evening and they found her neighbour so ill that a doctor had to be called and she was admitted to hospital. Helen was a young friend on whom Jean knew she could always call. She often visited Jean and generally took a responsible interest in her affairs, so she felt a real sense of loss when Jean left Edinburgh.

In mid-1995 she was contemplating a holiday with some friends to Guernsey where William Campbell had made his home but wrote, "I am embarrassed to write this note but I have cancelled my holiday in Guernsey once more. I was quite ill last night and felt very weak this morning. So I went to see the Doctor and I am to see a specialist. I am feeling better already! My best friends are astonished at my 'capers', my change of mind!"

About 1997 she began to be concerned about her health and to think, reluctantly, of leaving Edinburgh. During these days when she was beginning to feel her frailty, she often quoted, "Have faith in God". In 1999 she had to go into hospital for an operation and her health slowly deteriorated. She decided to go into Ballifeary Home in Inverness, run by the Free Presbyterian Church. The huge task of packing up and arranging for the move was undertaken in the final months by Rhoda, Ishbel and Katie, who was home on leave. They

Ballifeary House, Inverness.

A HEART FOR AFRICA

took it in turns to stay with her for a few weeks at a time as she no longer had the necessary strength for such hard work and she greatly appreciated their help. This was a sad task for her to oversee as her home and possessions held precious memories.

She moved to Inverness in November 1999 and was so pleased that the Matron was none other than Catherine, daughter of Rev John Tallach. Of course the friendship had been kept up over the intervening years and Catherine looked after her lovingly. She and Ishbel were specially close to her during the last weeks of her life.

It gave her particular pleasure that among the residents was Mrs Betty Tallach, a sister of Rev James Fraser and mother of Dr James Tallach who had spent several years at Mbuma. Their friendship went a long way back. For the first months she kept reasonably well and even thought of buying a place of her

Taken with Rev Lachlan Macleod. Translated from Uig, Lewis, he was inducted to the Greenock congregation in 1965. Retiring to Dingwall after almost 40 years' service, he predeceased Jean Nicolson by 18 months.

own. She enjoyed being asked out to meals but tired more easily and was less the life and soul of the company. Catherine wrote to William, "It was difficult to know just how long she would be with us, as she would 'pick up' and be so cheery and chatty and entertain us all with her cheery stories. The next day she could be very tired and a bit flat, but then pick up again and be as cheery as ever . . . she was already so very weak – weaker than we really realised, because she never really complained. She was a very brave uncomplaining person and a most gracious loving friend. She loved all the staff in Ballifeary, and they all loved her and admired tremendously her shining Christian spirit and witness. . . . . She was young at heart and loved having young folk around and they appreciated her and her kindness."

When she was very weak and tired and not able to concentrate much she jotted down several verses of Scripture on a sheet of paper which she kept near at hand. Every now and then she would pick it up and repeat the verses to herself.

•

"Thou with Thy counsel while I live
wilt me conduct and guide
and to Thy glory afterward
receive me to abide.
Whom have I in the heavens high
but Thee, O Lord, alone?"
And there is none whom I desire . . .

•

"I will never leave thee nor forsake thee." Fulfil it, O Lord, daily for Thine own great name's sake.

A multitude of people all dressed the same as if the sun was shining on them. On the other side was . . . .

We are dying daily "and on thy side, thou son of Jesse".

•

Among many visitors Rev Alfred MacDonald called some weeks before she died. It was his last visit and she greatly appreciated the time of fellowship they had together. In early May, Rev Donald Ross came to see her and quoted, "Him that cometh unto Me I will in no wise cast out." When he came back some days later she said, "I am resting on that text."

Late on Saturday evening, 20 May 2000, she died and the following Friday she was buried in Grange Cemetery in Edinburgh, the funeral service being taken by Rev Hugh Cartwright. An obituary by Rev John MacLeod in the *Free Presbyterian Magazine* concludes with the words, "Jean Nicolson faced death in full possession of her faculties and with marvellous calmness and equanimity. She was aware that the time of her departure was at hand and, when the moment arrived, it was for her, we fully believe, a parting to be with Christ 'which is far better'. Her latter end was peace. She has gone from us to be now among the spirits of just men made perfect, to join those whom she loved in time and in whose company she took delight."

A passage from *Pilgrim's Progress* follows in which is described Mr Valiant for Truth's crossing of the river: "When the day that he must go hence was come, many accompanied him to the river side; into which as he went, he said, 'Death, where is thy sting?' And as he went deeper, he said, 'Grave, where is thy victory?' So he passed over, and all the trumpets sounded for him on the other side."

IN LOVING MEMORY
OF
JEAN NICOLSON
BORN 8th JANUARY 1908
DIED 20th MAY 2000
AFTER A LIFETIME OF
DEVOTED TEACHING
AND OTHER SERVICE IN
THE MISSION OF THE
FREE PRESBYTERIAN
CHURCH OF SCOTLAND
AT INGWENYA ZIMBABWE

Jean Nicolson's grave in Grange Cemetery, Edinburgh.